PUBLISHED by PARABLES
Earthly Stories with a Heavenly Meaning

Pathways To The Past

Each volume stands alone as an Individual Book
Each volume stands together with others
to enhance the value of your collection

Build your Personal, Pastoral or Church Library
Pathways To The Past contains an ever-expanding list of
Christendom's most influential authors

Augustine of Hippo
Athanasius
E. M. Bounds
John Bunyan
Robert Lewis Darby
Brother Lawrence
Jessie Penn-Lewis
Bernard of Clairvaux
Andrew Murray
Watchman Nee
Arthur W. Pink
Thomas Watson
Hannah Whitall Smith
R. A. Torrey
A. W. Tozer
Jean-Pierre de Caussade
And many, many more.

How To Bring Men To Christ

By

R. A. Torrey

How To Bring Men To Christ
R. A.. Torrey,

Published By Parables
September, 2018

ISBN
Printed in the United States of America

How To Bring Men To Christ

By

R. A. Torrey

PREFACE

This book is written because it seems to be needed. The author has been repeatedly requested by Ministers, Y. M. C. A. Secretaries, Christian Workers, and his own students to put into a permanent and convenient shape the substance of what he has said at Conventions, Summer Schools and in the class–room on personal work. The time has come to yield to these requests. Never before in the history of the Church were there so many who desire to win others to Christ. The good work done by the Young People's Society of Christian Endeavor is in no other direction so evident as in the many thousands of young people in this land who to–day are on fire with a desire to win souls. But while they desire to do this work, many do not know how. This little book aims to tell them. There are several well–known and valuable manuals of texts to be used with inquirers, but this book is intended not only to point out passages to be used but to show how to use them, illustrating this use by cases from 4actual experience. It is hoped that from a careful study of these pages any earnest Christian can learn how to do efficient work in bringing others to the Saviour.

CHAPTER I.

THE GENERAL CONDITIONS OF SUCCESS IN BRINGING MEN TO CHRST

There are certain general conditions, the fulfillment of which is absolutely essential to real success in bringing men to Christ. These conditions, fortunately, are few and simple and such as any one can meet.

1. The one who would have real success in bringing others to Christ must himself be A THOROUGHLY CONVERTED PERSON. Jesus said to Peter, "When thou art converted strengthen thy brethren." He was in no position to help his brethren until he himself, after his cowardly denial, had turned again to his Lord with his whole heart. If we would bring others to Christ we must turn away from all sin, and worldliness and selfishness with our whole heart, yielding to Jesus the absolute lordship over our thoughts, purposes and 8actions. If there is any direction in which we are seeking to have our own way and not letting Him have His own way in our lives, our power will be crippled and men lost that we might have saved. The application of this principle to the numerous questions that come up in the life of every young Christian as to whether he should do this or that, each individual can settle for himself if Christ's honor and not his own pleasure is upper–most in his mind and if he looks honestly to God to guide him.

2. The one who would have real success in bringing others to Christ must have a LOVE FOR SOULS, i. e. a longing for the salvation of the lost. If we have no love for souls, our efforts will be mechanical and powerless. We may know how to approach men and what to say to them, but there will be no power in what we say and it will not touch

the heart. But if like Paul we have "great heaviness and unceasing pain in our hearts" for the unsaved, there will be an earnestness in our tone and manner that will impress the most careless. Furthermore if we have a love for souls we will be on the constant watch for opportunities to speak with the unsaved and will find opportunities on the street, in the store, in 9the home, on the cars and everywhere that would otherwise have entirely escaped our notice.

But how is one to get a love for souls? This question is easily answered. First of all, a love for souls like every other grace of Christian character, is the work of the Holy Spirit. If then we are conscious that we do not have that love for souls that we should have, the first thing to do is to go to God and humbly confess this lack in our lives and ask Him by His Holy Spirit to supply that which we so sorely need, and expect Him to do it (1 Jno. v. 14, 15; Phil. iv. 19). In the second place Jesus Christ had an intense love for souls (Matt. xxiii. 37; Luke xix. 10), and intimate and constant companionship with Him will impart to our lives this grace which was so prominent in His. In the third place feelings are the outcome of thoughts. If we desire any given feeling in our lives we should dwell upon the thoughts which are adapted to produce that feeling. If any saved person will dwell long enough upon the peril and wretchedness of any man out of Christ and the worth of his soul in God's sight as seen in the death of God's Son to save him, a feeling of intense desire 10for that man's salvation is almost certain to follow. In the fourth place, reflection upon our own ruined and unhappy condition without Christ and the great sacrifice that Christ made to save us, is sure to fill our hearts with a desire to bring others to the Saviour we have found.

3. The one who would have real success in bringing men to Christ must have a WORKING KNOWLEDGE OF THE BIBLE. The Word of God is the sword of the Spirit (Eph. vi. 17). It is the instrument God uses to convict of sin, to reveal Christ and to regenerate men. If we would work

together with God, the Bible is the instrument upon which we must rely and which we must use in bringing men to Christ. We must know how to use the Bible so as (1) to show men their need of a Saviour, (2) to show them Jesus as the Saviour they need, (3) to show them how to make this Saviour their own Saviour, (4) to meet the difficulties that stand in the way of their accepting Christ. A large part of the following pages will be devoted to imparting this knowledge.

4. The one who would have real success in bringing men to Christ must PRAY MUCH. Solid work in soul winning must be accompanied 11by prayer at every step. (1). We must pray God to lead us to the right persons to approach. God does not intend that we speak to every one we meet. If we try to do it, we will waste much valuable time in speaking to those whom we cannot help, that we might have used in speaking to those to whom we could have done much good. God alone knows the one to whom He intends us to speak, and we must ask Him to point him out to us, and, expect Him to do it. (Acts viii. 29). (2). We must pray God to show us just what to say to those to whom He leads us. After all our study of the passages to be used in dealing with the various classes of men, we shall need God's guidance in each specific case. Every experienced worker will testify to the many instances in which God has led them to use some text of Scripture that they would not otherwise have used but which proved to be just the one needed. (3). We must pray God to give power to that which He has given us to say. We need not only a message from God but power from God to send the message home. Most workers have to learn this lesson by humiliating experiences. They sit down beside an unsaved man and reason and plead 12and bring forth texts from the word of God, but the man does not accept Christ. At last it dawns upon them that they are trying to convert the man in their own strength and then they lift an humble and earnest prayer to God for his strength, and God hears and in a short time this "very difficult case" has settled the matter and is rejoicing in Christ. (4). We must pray God to carry on

the work after our work has come to an end. After having done that which seems to have been our whole duty in any given instance, whatever may have been the apparent issue of our work, whether successful or unsuccessful, we should definitely commit the case to God in prayer. If there is anything the average worker in this hurrying age needs to have impressed upon him, it is the necessity of more prayer. By praying more we will not work any less and we will accomplish vastly more.

5. The one who would have real success in bringing men to Christ must be "BAPTIZED WITH THE HOLY GHOST." "Ye shall receive power after that the Holy Ghost, is come upon you," said Jesus to his disciples after having given them the great commission to go out and bring men to Himself. The supreme condition of soul winning power is the same 13to–day: "after that the Holy Ghost is come upon you." A later chapter will be given to a study of what "the Baptism of the Holy Ghost" is and how any Christian can obtain it.

CHAPTER II.

HOW TO BEGIN

When God has led us to think that He wishes us to make an effort to lead some given individual to Christ, the first question that confronts us is, "How shall I begin?" If the person has gone into an inquiry room, or remained to an after–meeting, or even if they are merely present at prayer–meeting, Sunday–school or other ordinary service of the church, it is comparatively easy. You can then ask him if he is a Christian, or if he would not like to be a Christian, or why he is not a Christian or some other direct and simple question that will lead inevitably to a conversation along this line. But if the person is one in whom you have become interested outside the religious meeting and who is perhaps an entire stranger, it does not at first sight appear so simple, and yet it is not so very difficult. The person can be engaged in conversation on some general topic or on something suggested by passing events, and 15soon brought around to the great subject. Christ's conversation with the woman of Samaria in the 4th chapter of John is a very instructive illustration of this. Oftentimes even in dealing with entire strangers it is well to broach the subject at once and ask them if they are Christians or if they are saved or some similar question. If this is done courteously and earnestly it will frequently set even careless people to thinking and result in their conversion. It is astonishing how often one who undertakes this work in humble dependence upon God and under His direction, finds the way prepared and how seldom he receives any rebuff. One day the writer met a man on one of the most crowded streets of Chicago. As I passed him the impulse came to speak to him about the Saviour. Stopping a moment and asking God to show me if the impulse was from Him, I turned around and followed the man. I overtook him in the middle of the street, laid my hand upon his shoulder and said: “My friend, are you a Christian?” He started and said: “That's a strange question to ask a man.” I said, “I know it, and I do not ask that question of every stranger, but God put it into my heart to ask it of you.” He then told me that his cousin was a minister 16and had been urging this very matter upon him, that he himself was a graduate of Amherst college, but had been ruined by drink. After further conversation we separated but later the man accepted Christ as his Saviour.

It is often best to win a person's confidence and affection before broaching the subject. It is well to select some one and then lay your plans to win him to Christ. Cultivate his acquaintance, show him many attentions and perform many acts of kindness great and small and at last when the fitting moment arrives take up the great question. An old and thorough going infidel in Chicago was in this way won to Christ by a young woman, who found him sick and alone. She called day after day and showed him many kindnesses and as the consumption fastened itself more firmly upon him she spoke to him of the Saviour and had the joy of seeing him accept Christ.

A wisely chosen tract placed in the hand of the one with whom you wish to speak will often lead easily and naturally to the subject. One day I was riding on a train and praying that God would use me to lead some one to His Son. A young lady, daughter of a minister, with whom I had had some conversation 17on this subject came in with a friend and took the seat immediately in front of me. I took out a little bundle of tracts and selected one that seemed adapted for the purpose and handed it to her and asked her to read it. As she read, I prayed. When she had finished, I leaned over and asked her what she thought about it. She was deeply moved and I asked her if she would not accept Christ right there. Her difficulties were soon met and answered and she accepted Christ. As she left the train she thanked me very heartily for what I had done for her.

You will often meet some one whose face tells the story of unhappiness or discontent: in such a case it is easy to ask the person if he is happy and when he answers "no" you can say, "I can tell you of one who will make you happy if you will only take Him." Skill in beginning a conversation will come with practice. One may be rather awkward about it at first but as we go on we will acquire facility.

When the subject is once opened the first thing to find out is where the person with whom you are dealing stands; then you will know how to wisely treat his case. In the chapters immediately following this all the 18classes of men one is likely to meet will be given, and the first point to be ascertained is to which class any given individual belongs. But how can we find out to which class any person belongs? First. By asking him questions. Such questions as "Are you a Christian?" "Are you saved?" "Do you know that your sins are forgiven?" "Have you eternal life?" "Are you confessing Christ openly before the world?" "Are you a friend of Jesus?" "Have you been born again?" One may answer these questions untruthfully, either through ignorance or a desire to mislead you. Nevertheless, their answers and the manner of them will show you a great deal about their real state. Second. By watching his face. A man's face will often reveal that which his words try to conceal. Any one who cultivates the study of the faces of those with whom he deals will soon be able to tell in many instances the exact state of those with whom they are dealing irrespective of anything they may say. Third. By the Holy Spirit. The Holy Spirit if we only look to Him to do it will often flash into our minds a view of the man's position, and just the scripture he needs.

When we have learned where the person 19with whom we are dealing stands, the next thing to do is to lead him as directly as we can to accept Jesus Christ, as his personal Savior and Master. We must always bear in mind that the primary purpose of our work, is not to get persons to join the church or to give up their bad habits or to do anything else than this, to accept Jesus Christ, as their Saviour—the one who bore their sins in his own body on the tree and through whom they can have immediate and entire forgiveness,—and as their Master to whom they surrender absolutely the guidance of their thoughts, feelings, purposes and actions. Having led any one to thus accept Christ the next step will be to show him from God's word that he has forgiveness of sins and eternal life. Acts x. 43; xiii. 39; Jno. iii. 36; v. 24, will answer for this purpose. The next step will be to show him how to make a success of the Christian life upon which he has entered. How to do this will be told later. Each person is to be led to accept Christ through a use of the word of God. In the chapters that immediately follow this we will try to show what specific portions of the word to use in given cases and how to use them.

CHAPTER III.

DEALING WITH THE INDIFFERENT OR CARELESS

One of the classes of men most frequently met with, is The Indifferent, or Careless. There are several ways of dealing with them. One is to show them their need of a Saviour. A good verse to use for this purpose is Romans iii. 23. Get the person with whom you are dealing to read the verse, "For all have sinned and come short of the glory of God." Then say to him: "Who have sinned?" "All." "Who does that include?" and keep up the questioning until he says, "It includes me." Then ask him what it is that he has done, and keep at it until he comes out plainly and says: "I have sinned and come short of the glory of God." This is likely to make him feel his need of a Saviour. Another good verse to use is Isaiah liii. 6. After the verse has been read, ask him who it is that has gone astray and by a series of questions bring him to the point where he will say, "I have gone astray." Then 21ask him what kind of a sheep one is that has "gone astray" and hold him to it until he says "a lost sheep." "What are you then?" "Lost." Then ask him what the Lord has done with his sin, and hold him to that point until he sees the truth of the verse, that God has laid his sin on Jesus Christ. Now, he is in a position for you to put to him the direct question: "Will you accept this Saviour upon whom the Lord has laid your sin?" Still another verse to use is Psalms cxxx. 3. When the verse has been read, ask him, "If the Lord marked iniquities could you stand?" In dealing with this class of men I use Matthew xxii. 37, 38 more frequently than any other passage of Scripture. Before having the person read the verse, it is well to ask him, "Do you know that you have committed the greatest sin that a man can commit?" In all probability he will answer, "No, I have not." Then ask him what he thinks the greatest sin a man can commit. When he has answered, say to him, Now let us see what God considers the greatest sin. Read the verses and ask him, "What is the first and greatest of the commandments?" Then ask him, "What then is the greatest sin?" He will soon answer that the violation of the first and greatest of the commandments 22must be the greatest sin. Ask him if he has kept that commandment and when he confesses, as sooner or later he must, that he has not, ask him of what he is guilty in the sight of God, and hold him to that point until he admits that he is guilty of committing the greatest sin that a man can commit. An illustration from life may help to make the use of this verse clear. I was dealing with a very bright young man who evidently had no deep sense of sin nor of his need of a Saviour. In fact when I asked if he was a Christian he said promptly that he always had been; but there was something in his manner that showed that he had no clear understanding of what it meant to be a Christian. I then asked if he had been born again and he did not even understand what I was talking about. I next asked if he knew he had committed the greatest sin that a man could possibly commit and he at once answered, "No, I never did in my life." I asked what he considered the greatest sin, and he replied "murder." I took my Bible and opened it to Matthew xxii. 37, 38, and asked him to read the verses, which he did. I then asked him, "If this is the first and greatest commandment, what must be the greatest sin?" He answered, "I suppose 23the breaking of that commandment." I then asked if he had always kept that commandment, if he had always loved God with all his heart, with all his soul, and with all his mind. If he had always put God first in everything. He replied that he had not. I then asked him, "Of what then are you guilty?" The Spirit of God carried the text home and with the greatest earnestness he replied, "I have committed the greatest sin that a man can commit, but I never saw it before in my life." Another verse that can be used with effect is John viii. 34.

After the man has read the verse, "Whosoever committeth sin is the servant of sin," ask him "what is one who commits sin?" Then ask him if he commits sin. Then put to him the direct question, "What are you then," and hold him to it until he says "the servant of sin." Then ask him if he does not desire to be delivered from that awful bondage. Hold him to this point until he sees his need of Jesus Christ as a Deliverer from the slavery of sin. The Holy Spirit has used Isaiah lvii. 21 to the salvation of many men who have been indifferent to the claims of the Gospel. After the verse, "There is no peace saith my God to the wicked," has been read slowly, thoughtfully, and earnestly, 24ask him who it is that says this. Then ask him if it is true; then ask him if it is true in his case. "Have you peace?" One night a careless young man was going out of one of our tents in Chicago and as he passed by me I took him by the hand and said to him, "You need the Saviour." He wanted to know why I thought so. I replied, "Because you have no peace." He said, "Yes I have." "No you have not." He then asked me how I knew that. I told him God said so and quoted the above passage. He tried to laugh it off and say the verse was not true in his case. Then he became angry and went out of the tent in a rage, but the next night I saw him kneeling with one of our workers in prayer and when he arose from his knees, the worker came over and said he wished to speak with me. As I approached him he held out his hand and said, "I wanted to beg your pardon for what I said last night; what you said was true, I didn't have peace." I asked him if he had now accepted the Saviour. He said he had.

Galatians iii. 10 is a verse which we very frequently use in our work in dealing with the Indifferent. After the one with whom you are dealing has read the verse, "For as many as are of the works of the law 25are under the curse; for it is written cursed is every one that continueth not in all things which are written in the book of the law to do them" ask him the question, "What is every one that continueth not in all things which are written in the book of the law to do them?"

When he answers, "Cursed," ask him if he has continued in all things which are written in the book of the law to do them and when he replies, "No, I have not," put to him the direct question, "What are you then?" and hold him to that point until he says, "I am under the curse." In very many cases the inquirer will be ready at once to be led to the thirteenth verse of the same chapter which shows how he may be saved from that curse under which he rests. Romans vi. 23 can often be used with good effect. "For the wages of sin is death." Ask "what are the wages of sin?" Then, "who earns those wages?" Then, "Are you a sinner?" "What wages then have you earned?" "Do you wish to take your wages?" John iii. 36 is a verse which can be used in a similar way. Ask the question, "Upon whom is it that the wrath of God abides?" Then, "Do you believe on the Son?" "What then abides upon you?" Then put the decisive question, "Are 26you willing to go away with the wrath of God abiding upon you?" 2 Thes. i. 7–9, and John viii. 24; Rev. xx. 15; xxi. 8; xiv. 10–11, set forth in a most impressive way the awful consequences of sin. If these verses are used they should be read with the deepest earnestness and solemnity and dwelt upon until the person with whom you are dealing realizes their terrible import.

There is another way to arouse a man from his indifference, and that is by showing what Jesus has done for him. I have found Isaiah liii. 5–6 more effectual for this purpose than any other passage in the Bible. An incident from life will illustrate its use. A lady had asked prayers for her daughter, a young woman about twenty years of age. At the close of the services I stepped up to the daughter and asked her if she would not accept Jesus Christ as her Saviour at once. She stamped her foot in anger and said, "My mother should have known better than to do that; she knows it will only make me worse." I asked her if she would not sit down for a few minutes and as soon as we were seated I opened my Bible to this passage and began to read, "But he was wounded for our transgressions, he was bruised for our iniquities; 27the chastisement of our peace was upon him; and with his stripes we are healed. All we like sheep have gone astray; we have turned every one to his own way; and the Lord hath laid on him the iniquity of us all." I made no comment upon the verses whatever, but the Spirit of God carried them home and tears began to roll down the cheeks of the young woman. She did not come out as a Christian that night but did shortly afterward. It is well in using these verses, whenever it is possible, to get the inquirer to change the pronoun from the plural to the singular. "He was wounded for my transgressions; he was bruised for my iniquities, etc." John iii. 16 can be used in a similar way. I was talking one night to one who was apparently most indifferent and hardened. She told me the story of her sin, with seemingly very little sense of shame, and when I urged her to accept Christ, she simply refused. I put a Bible in her hands and asked her to read this verse. She began to read, "God so loved the world that He gave His only begotten Son," and before she had finished reading the verse she had broken into tears, softened by the thought of God's wondrous love to her. First Peter ii. 24 is a verse of similar character. 28Ask the inquirer whose sins they were that Jesus bore in his own body on the tree, and hold him to it until he says, "My sins." 1 Peter i. 18–19; Luke xxii. 44; Matt. xxvii. 46, are useful as bringing out in detail what Christ has suffered for us.

There is still another way to arouse indifferent persons, and that is by showing them that the one damning sin is that of which they themselves are guilty—the sin of rejecting Jesus Christ. Heb. x. 28–29 is very effective for this purpose. John xvi. 9; iii. 18, 19, 20, and Acts ii. 36 can also be used.

Oftentimes you will meet one who is not willing to sit down and let you deal with him in this deliberate way. In that case the only thing to do is to look up to God for guidance and power and give him some pointed verse in great earnestness, such for example as Heb. x. 28–29; Romans

vi. 23; John iii. 36; Isaiah lvii. 21, and leave it for the Spirit of God to carry the truth home to his heart. A passing shot of this kind has often resulted in the salvation of a soul. The passages given above can be wisely used with one who is not altogether indifferent or careless but who has not a sufficiently deep sense of sin and need to be ready to accept the Gospel.

CHAPTER IV.

DEALING WITH THOSE WHO ARE ANXIOUS TO BE SAVED BUT DO NOT KNOW HOW

There is a very large class of persons who are anxious to be saved but simply do not know how. It is not difficult to lead this class of persons to Christ. Perhaps no other passage in the Bible is more used for this purpose than Isaiah liii. 6. It makes the way of salvation very plain. Read the first part of the verse to the inquirer, "All we like sheep have gone astray, we have turned every one to his own way." Then ask, "Is that true of you," and when he has thought it over and said "yes," then say to him, "Now let us see what God has done with your sins," and read the remainder of the verse, "And the Lord hath laid on him the iniquity of us all." "What then is it necessary for you to do to be saved?" Very soon he can be led to see that all that it is necessary for him to do is to accept the sin bearer whom God has provided. Some years ago I noticed in a meeting a white–haired 30man who did not stand up with the Christians. At the close of the service I walked down to him and said, "Are you not a Christian?" He said he was not. I was sure he was interested, so I put to him the direct question, "Would you become a Christian to–night if I would show you the way?" and he replied that he would. We sat down together and I opened my Bible to Isaiah liii. 6 and read the first part of the verse, "All we like sheep have gone astray, we have turned every one to his own way." I then said to him, "Is that true of you?" and he answered "yes." "Now," I said, "let us read the rest of the verse, 'And the Lord hath laid on him the iniquity of us all.'" "What has the Lord done," I said, "with your sins?" He thought a moment and said "he has laid them on Christ." "What then" I said "is all that you have to do to be saved?" and he replied quite promptly, "Accept him." "Well," I said, "will you accept him to–night?" He said, "I will." "Let us then kneel down and tell God so." We knelt down and I led in prayer and he followed in a very simple way telling God that he was a sinner but that he believed that He had laid his sins upon Jesus Christ, and asking God for Christ's sake to forgive his sins. When he 31had finished I asked him if he thought God had heard his prayer and that his sins were forgiven, and he said "yes." I then asked him if he would begin to lead a Christian life at once, set up the family altar and openly confess Christ before the world, and he replied that he would. Some months after I met his pastor and made inquiries about him and found that he had gone to his home in a distant village, set up the family altar and united with the church together with his son, the only remaining member of the family out of Christ. Apparently all that this man was waiting for was for some one to make the way of salvation plain to him. I sometimes put it this way in using this verse: "There are two things which a man needs to know and one thing he needs to do in order to be saved. What he needs to know is, first, that he is a lost sinner and this verse tells him that; second, that Christ is an all–sufficient Saviour and this verse tells him that. What he needs to do is simply to accept this all–sufficient Saviour whom God has provided." John i. 12 brings out this thought very clearly, "As many as received him to them gave he power to become the sons of God, even to them that believe on 32his name." After the verse has been read you can ask the one with whom you are dealing, "To whom is it that God gives the power to become the sons of God?" "As many as receive him." What must you then do to become a son of God? "Receive him." Well, will you receive him as your Saviour and as your master now? Isaiah lv. 7; Acts xvi. 31; John iii. 16 and iii. 36 are all useful in making the way of salvation plain. John iii. 14 compared with Numbers xxi. 8 and the following verses, can often be used with good effect. When they are used you should lead the inquirer to see just what the serpent–bitten Israelite had to do to be saved—that he had simply to look at the brazen serpent lifted up upon the pole—then show him that the sin–bitten man has to do simply the same thing—look at Christ lifted up on the Cross for his sins. Romans i. 16 is another excellent verse to use. It makes the way of salvation very clear. You can ask the inquirer whom it is, according to his verse, that the Gospel saves, and he will see that it is "every one that believeth." Then ask him, "What then is all that is necessary for one to do in order to be saved," and he will see that it is simply to believe. Then ask him "believe what," and 33the answer is "the Gospel." The next question that naturally arises is, what is the Gospel? This is answered by 1 Cor. xv.; 1–4. These verses show what the Gospel is, "that Christ died for our sins according to the Scriptures; that he was buried and that he rose the third day according to the scriptures" and this is what he must believe in order to be saved. He must believe from his heart that Christ died for his sins and that he rose again. Then ask the inquirer, "do you believe that Christ died for your sins? do you believe that he rose again?" If he says that he does, ask him if he will make this a heart faith and get down and ask God for Christ's sake, to forgive his sins and believe he does it because he says so, and then trust in the living Saviour to save him day by day from the power of sin. Romans x. 9–10 also makes the way of salvation clear to many minds where other verses fail. Romans x. 13 makes it, if possible, more simple still. This shows that all that a man has to do to be saved is to "call upon the name of the Lord." You can ask the inquirer "Are you ready now and here to get down and call upon the name of the Lord for salvation and to believe that God saves you because he says he will?" The way of salvation can be 34made plain by the use of Exodus xii. 7, 13, 23. These verses show that it was the blood that made the Israelites safe and just so it is to–day the blood that makes us safe, and when God sees the blood he passes over us. The only thing for us to do is to get behind the blood. Then show the inquirer that the way to be behind the blood is by simple faith in Jesus Christ. Luke xviii. 10–14 is exceedingly useful in showing what a man may have and yet be lost (the Pharisee) and what a man may lack and yet be saved (the Publican) and that all that a man has to do to be saved is simply to do as the Publican did, that is take the sinner's place and cry to God for mercy and then he will go down to his house justified. This passage can be used in the following manner to make the meaning more clear. Ask the inquirer, "Which one of these two (the Pharisee or the Publican) went down to his house justified?" Then ask him, "What did the Publican do that the Pharisee did not do, that brought him the forgiveness of his sins while the Pharisee went out of the Temple unforgiven?" When he studies the passage he will soon see that what the Publican did was simply to take the sinner's place before God and cry for mercy and that as soon as he 35did this he was "justified" or forgiven. Then you can ask him, "What is all that it is necessary for you to do to find forgiveness?" Then ask him, "Will you do it now and here?" and when he has done so ask him if he believes God's word and if he is going down to his house justified. What saving faith is, is beautifully illustrated by Luke vii. 48–50. The fiftieth verse tells us that this woman had saving faith. Now ask the inquirer, "What was the faith she had," and show him that her faith was simply such faith that Jesus could and would forgive her sins, that she came to him to do it. This is saving faith. Galatians iii. 10–13 also makes the way of salvation very simple. The tenth verse shows the sinner's position before accepting Christ—"under the curse." The thirteenth verse shows what Christ has done—has been made a curse for us. What the sinner had to do is, evidently, simply to accept Christ.

CHAPTER V.

DEALING WITH THOSE WHO ARE ANXIOUS TO BE SAVED AND KNOW HOW, BUT WHO HAVE DIFFICULTIES

A very large number of persons whom we try to lead to Christ, we will find are really anxious to be saved and know how, but are confronted with difficulties which they deem insurmountable.

1. One of the difficulties is, "I am too great a sinner." 1 Tim. i. 15 meets this fully. One Sunday morning a man who had led a wild and wandering life and who had recently lost $35,000 and been separated from his wife, said to me in response to my question, why he was not Christian, "I am too great a sinner to be saved." I turned at once to 1 Tim. i. 15. "This is a faithful saying and worthy of all acceptation, that Christ Jesus came into the world to save sinners, of whom I am chief." He quickly replied, "well, I am the chief of sinners." "Well," I said, "that verse means you then." He replied, "It is a precious 37promise." I said, "Will you accept it now?" and he said, "I will." Then I said, "Let us kneel down and tell God so," and we knelt down and he confessed to God his sins, and asked God for Christ's sake to forgive him his sins. I asked him if he had really accepted Christ and he said he had. I asked him if he really believed that he was saved and he said he did. He took an early opportunity of confessing Christ. He left the city in a short time but I was able to follow him. He became a most active Christian, working at his business day times but engaged in some form of Christian work every night in the week. He was reunited to his wife and adopted a little child out of an orphan asylum

and had a happy Christian home. Luke xix. 10 is also a very useful passage to use in dealing with this class of men; especially useful when a man says, “I am lost.” You can say, “I have a passage intended expressly for you. If you really mean what you say, you are just the man Jesus is seeking. ‘For the Son of man is come to seek and save that which was lost.’” Romans v. 6–8 is a very effective passage. I stopped a man one night as he was hurrying out of a meeting. Laying my hand on his shoulder I said “Did you not hold your hand 38up to–night for prayers?” He said “yes.” I said, “Why then are you hurrying away? Do you know God loves you?” He replied, “You do not know who you are talking to.” “I do not care who I am talking to but I know God loves you.” He said: “I am the meanest thief in Minneapolis.” I said “If you are the meanest thief in Minneapolis, then I know God loves you,” and I opened my Bible to Romans v. 8. “But God commendeth his love toward us in that while we were yet sinners Christ died for us.” “Now,” I said, “If you are the meanest thief in Minneapolis, you are a sinner, and this verse tells that God loves sinners.” The man broke down and going into another room with me told me his story. He was just out of confinement for crime; had started out that very night to commit what he said would have been one of the most daring burglaries ever committed in the city of Minneapolis; with his two companions in crime he was passing a corner where he happened to hear an open–air meeting going on and stopped a few minutes to hear and in spite of the protests and oaths of his companions stayed through the meeting and went with us to the Mission. After telling me his story we kneeled in prayer. Through 39tears he cried to God for mercy, having been led by God’s precious promise to believe that God loved a sinner even as vile as he. Matt. ix. 12, 13; Romans x. 13 (Emphasize “whosoever”); John iii. 16 (Emphasize the “whosoever”); Isaiah i. 18; 1 John iv. 14; John ii. 1–2; Isaiah xliv. 22; Isaiah xliii. 25 are also useful passages in dealing with this class of men. Isaiah i. 18 and Ps. li. 14 are especially useful in dealing with men who have committed murder. Never tell any one that his sins are not great. It is well sometimes to say to these men, "Yes, your sins are great, greater than you think, but they have all been settled" and show them Isaiah liii. 6; 1 Peter ii. 24. A woman once came to me in great agitation. After many ineffectual attempts she was at last able to unburden her heart. Fourteen years before she had killed a man and had borne the memory of the act upon her conscience until it had almost driven her crazy. When she told the story to another Christian and myself, we turned to Isaiah liii. 6. After reading the verse very carefully to her, I asked her what the Lord had done with her sin. After a few moments' deep and anxious thought she said, "He has laid it on Christ," I took a book in my hand. "Now," I said "let 40my right hand represent you, and my left hand Christ, and this book your sin." I laid the book upon my right hand and I said: "Where is your sin now?" She said "On me." "Now," I said, "what has God done with it?" She said "Laid it on Christ," and I laid the book over on the other hand. "Where is your sin now?" I asked. It was long before she could summon courage to answer, and then with a desperate effort she said, "On Christ." I said, "then is it on you any longer?" Slowly the light came into her face and she burst out with a cry, "No, it is on Him, it is on Christ." John i. 29; Acts x. 43; Heb. vii. 25, are also helpful texts in dealing with this class of men.

2. Another difficulty we frequently meet with, is "I can't hold out," or "I am afraid of failure." 1 Peter i. 5 is useful in showing that we are not to keep ourselves but are "kept by the power of God." John x. 28, 29 shows that the safety of the one who accepts Christ does not depend upon his "holding out" but upon the keeping power of the Father and the Son. 2 Tim. i. 12 shows that it is Christ's business and not ours to keep that which is entrusted to him and that he is able to do it. Isaiah xli. 10, 13 are also 41helpful. Jude 24 shows that whether we can keep from falling or not, Christ is able to keep us from falling. 2 Chron. xxxii. 7, 8; Romans xiv. 4; 2 Thes. iii. 3, are also good texts to use. 1 Cor. x. 13 is

especially useful when one is afraid that some great temptation will overtake him and he will fall.

3. Another difficulty very similar to the preceding one, is "I am too weak." With such a person, use 2 Cor. xii. 9, 10. Ask him "where is it that Christ's strength is made perfect?" When he answers "in weakness," tell him "then the weaker you are in your own strength the better." Philippians iv. 13 shows that however weak we may be, we can do all things through Christ which strengtheneth us. 1 Cor. x. 13 will show that God knows all about our weakness and will not permit us to be tempted above our strength.

4. "I cannot give up my evil ways or bad habits." Gal. vi. 7, 8, will show them that they must give them up or perish. Philippians iv. 13 will show them that they can give them up in Christ's strength. It is an excellent plan to point the one who fears that he cannot give up his bad habits, to Christ, as a risen Saviour, 1 Cor. xv. 3, 4. A man once came to me and said: "I come to you to 42know if there is any way I can get power to overcome my evil habits." He told me his story; he had been converted in childhood but had come to Chicago, fallen in with evil companions and gone down, and now could not break away from his sins. I said to him: "You know only half the gospel, the gospel of a crucified Saviour. Through trusting in the crucified Saviour you found pardon. But Jesus Christ is also a risen Saviour, 1 Cor. xv. 4, 'All power is given unto Him,' Matt. xxviii. 18. He has power to give you victory over your evil habits. Do you believe that?" He said, "yes." "You trusted," I continued, "in the crucified Christ and found pardon, did you not?" "Yes," he replied. "Now," I said, "will you trust the risen Christ to save you from the power of your sins?" "Yes, I will." "Let us kneel down then, and tell him so." We knelt and talked it all over with the Saviour. When he arose his very countenance was changed. "I am so glad I came," he said. Some time after I received a letter from him telling me how he found constant victory through trusting in the risen Christ.

5. "I will be persecuted if I become a Christian." Never tell any one that he will not be persecuted, but show him from such passages 43as 2 Tim. ii. 12; 2 Tim. iii. 12; Matt. v. 10, 11, 12; Mark viii. 35; Acts xiv. 22, that persecution is the only path to Glory. Show them from Romans viii. 18 that the sufferings of this present time are not worthy to be compared with the Glory which shall be revealed in us. Show them from Acts v. 41; 1 Peter ii. 20, 21, that it is a privilege to be persecuted for Christ's sake. Heb. xii. 2, 3 is useful in showing them where to look for victory in persecution.

6. "It will hurt my business," or "I can't be a Christian in my present business." Point such an one to Mark viii. 36. This will show him that it is better to lose his business than to lose his soul. After this thought has been sufficiently impressed upon his mind, show him Matt. vi. 32, 33 which contains God's promise that if we put God and His kingdom first, that He will provide for all our real temporal needs. Matt. xvi. 24–27; Luke xii. 16–21; xvi. 24–26 are also very effective passages to use with this class.

7. "Too much to give up." Mark viii. 36 will show them that they had better give up everything than to lose their soul. Philippians iii. 7, 8; Ps. xvi. 11 will show them that what they give up is nothing compared with what 44they get. Ps. lxxxiv. 11; Romans viii. 32 will show them that God will not ask them to give up any good thing; in other words, that the only things God asks them to give up are the things that are hurting them. A young woman once refused to come to the Saviour saying, "There is too much to give up." "Do you think God loves you?" I answered. "Certainly." "How much do you think he loves you?" She thought a moment and answered, "Enough to give his son to die for me." "Do you think, if God loved you enough to give his son to die for you, he will ask you to give up anything it is for your good to keep?" "No." "Do you wish to keep anything that it is not for your good to keep?" "No." "Then you had better come to Christ at once."

And she did. 1 John ii. 17; Luke xii. 16–21 will show them how worthless are the things which they are trying to keep.

8. “The Christian life is too hard.” Say to the inquirer, “Let me show you from God’s word that you are mistaken about the Christian life being hard.” Then turn him to Matt. xi. 30; Prov. iii. 17; Ps. xvi. 11; 1 John v. 3, and show him that a Christian life is not hard but exceedingly pleasant. Then turn him to Prov. xiii. 15, and show him that it is the sinner’s life that is hard.

459. “I am afraid of my ungodly companions;” or “I will lose my friends if I take Christ.” Prov. xxix. 25 will show them the consequence of yielding to the fear of man and the security of the one who trusts in the Lord. Prov. xiii. 20 will show them the result of holding on to their companions, and Ps. i. 1 will show the blessedness of giving up evil companions. 1 John i. 3 shows how much better companionship one gets than he loses by coming to Christ.

10. “My heart is too hard.” Ezek. xxxvi. 26, 27, will show them that though their hearts are hard as stone, that will make no difference because God will give them a new heart.

11. “I have no feeling.” Ask the inquirer what kind of feeling he thinks he must have before he comes to Christ. If it is the peace of which Christians speak, show him from Gal. v. 22; Eph. i. 13; Acts v. 32; 1 Peter i. 8; Matt. x. 32, that this feeling is the result of accepting Christ and confessing Him, and that he cannot expect it until he accepts and confesses Christ. If the feeling which he thinks he must have is the feeling that he is a sinner, then show him by Is. lv. 7 that it is not the feeling that we are sinners that God demands, but a turning away from sin. Or, 46from Acts xvi. 31; John i. 12; that God does not ask us to feel that we are sinners but to confess that we are sinners and trust in Christ as a Saviour. Is. lv. 1; Rev. xxii. 17, will show the inquirer that all the feeling he needs is a desire for salvation.

It is often times well, however, with this class of inquirers to show them the passages for "The Indifferent" until they do feel that they are sinners.

12. "I am seeking Christ, but cannot find Him."

Jer. xxix. 13, shows that when we seek him with the whole heart we shall find him. Speaking with a woman one evening in an after–meeting she said to me, "I have been seeking Christ two years and cannot find Him." I replied, "I can tell you when you will find him." She looked at me in surprise and I turned to Jer. xxix. 13, and read "And ye shall seek me, and find me, when ye shall search for me with all your heart." "There," I said, "that shows you when you will find Christ. You will find him when you search for him with all your heart. Have you done that?" After a little thought she answered "No." "Well, then," I said, "let us kneel right down here now." She did this and in a few moments 47she was rejoicing in Christ. You can point one who has this difficulty to Luke xv. 1–10; xix. 10. These passages show that Jesus is seeking the sinner and you can say, "if you are really seeking Christ it will not take a seeking Saviour and a seeking sinner very long to find each other."

13. "I cannot believe."

In most cases where one says this the real difficulty which lies back of their inability to believe is unwillingness to forsake sin. John v. 44, is a good passage to use with such a one, or Is. lv. 7. In the use of the latter passage, hold the man's attention to the fact that all God asks of him is that he turn away from sin and turn to Him.

14. "God won't receive me," or "I have sinned away the day of grace," or "I am afraid I have committed the unpardonable sin."

The people who honestly say this, are as a rule about the most difficult class to deal with of any that you will meet.

John vi. 37, is the great text to use with them for it shows that Jesus will receive any one who will come to him. Hold him continually to that point, "Him that cometh to me I will in no wise cast out" and if they keep saying "He won't 48receive me" repeat the text, looking to the Spirit of God to carry the truth home. Many an utterly despondent soul has found light and peace through this verse in God's word. Rev. xxii. 17, is also useful as it shows that any one who will can have the water of life freely. Is. lv. 1, shows that any one who desires salvation can have it. Is. i. 18, shows that no matter how great a man's sins may be still here is pardon. Acts x. 43, and John iii. 16, that "whosoever" will believe upon Christ will find pardon and eternal life. Romans x. 13, shows that any one, no matter who or what he is, who will "call upon the name of the Lord shall be saved." It is well sometimes to turn to Heb. vi. 4–6, and Matt. xii. 31–32, and show the inquirer just what the unpardonable sin is and what its results are. Matt. xii. 31, 32, shows that it is blasphemy against the Holy Ghost and put it squarely to him, "have you ever blasphemed against the Holy Ghost?" Heb. vi. 4–6, shows that the difficulty is not in God's unwillingness to forgive, but in the man's unwillingness to repent and that any one who is concerned about his salvation evidently has not committed the unpardonable sin nor sinned away his day of grace. A little instruction 49along this line is often times all that is needed.

15. "It is too late."

When an inquirer says this, it is often times well to use 2 Cor. vi. 2, and tell him that God says, it is just the time. Luke xxiii. 39–43, is useful as showing that even at the last hour Jesus will hearken to the sinner's cry. 2 Peter iii. 9, will show that His will is that none should perish, but that He is delaying the judgment that He may save as many as will come. Deut. iv. 30, 31, is an especially helpful passage as it says "Even in the latter days" if thou turn to the Lord he will be merciful. Is. i. 18, and Rev. xxii. 17, can alone be used here.

CHAPTER VI.

DEALING WITH THOSE WHO ENTERTAIN FALSE HOPES

1. Among those who entertain false hopes, perhaps the largest class are those who expect to be saved by their righteous lives. These persons are easily known by such sayings as these, "I am doing the best I can." "I do more good than evil." "I am not a great sinner." "I have never done anything very bad." Gal. iii. 10, is an excellent passage to use, for it shows that all those who are trusting in their works are under the curse of the law and that there is no hope on the ground of the law for any one who does not "continue in all things which are written in the book of the law to do them." James ii. 10 is also useful. Gal. ii. 16, and Romans iii. 19, 20 are very effective by showing that by the deeds of the law there shall no flesh be justified in God's sight. Matt. v. 20—All these passages show the kind of righteousness God demands and that no man's righteousness 51comes up to God's standard, and that if a man wishes to be saved he must find some other means of salvation than by his own deeds. It is sometimes well in using these passages to say to the inquirer: "You do not understand the kind of righteousness that God demands or you would not talk as you do. Now let us turn to His word and see what kind of righteousness it is that God demands." There is another way of dealing with this class, by the use of such passages as Luke xvi. 15; Rom. ii. 16; 1 Sam. xvi. 7. These passages show that God looks at the heart. Hold the inquirer right to that point. Every man when brought face to face with that, must tremble because he knows that whatever his outward life may be, his heart will not stand the scrutiny of God's eye. No matter how selfrighteous a man is, we need not be discouraged for somewhere in the depths of every man's

heart is the consciousness of sin and all we have to do is to work away until we touch that point. Every man's conscience is on our side. Matt. xxii. 37, 38 can be used when a man says "I am doing the best I can, or doing more good than evil." Say to him, "You are greatly mistaken about that; so far from doing more good than evil, do you know that you have 52broken the first and greatest of God's laws?" Then show him the passage. Heb. xi. 6, John vi. 29, show that the one thing that God demands is faith and that without that it is impossible to please God, and John xvi. 9, shows that unbelief in Christ is the greatest sin. John iii. 36, shows that the question of eternal life depends solely upon a man's accepting or rejecting Jesus Christ, and Heb. x. 28, 29, that the sin which brings the heaviest punishment is that of treading under foot the Son of God. Before using this latter passage, it would be well to say, "You think you are very good, but do you know that you are committing the most awful sin in God's sight which a man can commit?" If he replies, "No," then say "Well let me show you from God's word that you are;" then turn to this passage and read it with great solemnity and earnestness.

2. Another class of those who entertain false hopes, are those who think "God is too good to damn anyone."

When any one says this, you can reply, "We know nothing of God's goodness but what we learn from the Bible, and we must go to that book to find out the character of God's goodness. Let us turn to Romans ii. 2, 4, 5." Having read the verses, you can say something 53like this, "Now, my friend, you see that the purpose of God's goodness is to lead you to repentance, not to encourage you in sin and when we trample upon his goodness, then we are treasuring up wrath against the day of wrath and revelation of the righteous judgment of God." John viii. 21, 24 and iii. 36, will show the man that however good God may be that he will reject all who reject His Son. Still another way to deal with these men is by showing them from John v. 40; 2 Peter iii.

9–11 or Ezek. xxxiii. 11, that it is not so much God who damns men as men who damn themselves in spite of God's goodness because they will not come to Christ and accept the life freely offered. You can say "God is not willing that any should perish and he offers life freely to you, but there is one difficulty in the way. Let us turn to John v. 40, and see what the difficulty is." Then read the passage: "Ye will not come to me that ye might have life," and say, "My friend here is the difficulty, you won't come; life is freely offered to you but if you will not accept it, you must perish." 2 Peter ii. 4–6, 9; Luke xiii. 3, show how the "good" God deals with persons who persist in sin. Sometimes this last passage can be effectively used in 54this way: "You say God is too good to damn any one. Now let us see what God Himself says in his word." Then turn to the passage and read, "Except ye repent, ye shall all likewise perish." Repeat the passage over and over again until it has been driven home.

3. A third class of those who entertain false hopes, are those who say "I am trying to be a Christian." John i. 12, will show them that it is not "trying" to be a Christian or "trying" to live a better life or "trying" to do anything that God asks of us, but simply to receive Jesus Christ, who did it all, and you can ask the inquirer, "will you now stop your trying and simply receive Jesus as Saviour?" Acts xvi. 31, shows that God does not ask us to try what we can do but trust Jesus and what He has done and will do. Romans iii. 23–25, shows that we are not to be justified by trying to do, "but freely by His grace, through the redemption that is in Christ Jesus" on the simple condition of faith.

4. Still another class of those who entertain false hopes are those who say, "I feel I am going to Heaven," or "I feel I am saved." Show them from John iii. 36 that it is not a question of what they feel but what God says, and what God says distinctly in his word is 55that, "He that believeth not on the Son, shall not see life, but the wrath of God abideth on him." One afternoon I was talking with a lady who a few

weeks before had lost her only child. At the time of the child's death she had been deeply interested, but her serious impressions had largely left her. I put to her the question, "Do you not wish to go where your little one has gone?" She replied at once "I expect to." "What makes you think you will?" I said. She replied, "I feel so, I feel that I will go to heaven when I die." I then asked her, if there was anything she could point to in the word of God which gave her a reason for believing that she was going to heaven when she died. "No," she said, "there is not." Then she turned and questioned me, saying, "Do you expect to go to heaven when you die?" "Yes," I replied, "I know I shall." "How do you know it?" she said. "Have you any word from God for it?" "Yes," I answered and turned her to John iii. 36. She was thus led to see the difference between a faith that rested upon her feelings and a faith that rested upon the word of God.

Luke xviii. 9–14, can also be used in the following way; you can say "there was a man in the Bible who felt he was all 56right, but was all wrong. Let me read you about him." Then read about the Pharisee who was so sure that he was all right, but who was all the time an unforgiven sinner; and make the inquirer see how untrustworthy our feelings are and what the ground of assurance is, viz: God's word. Prov. xiv. 12 can also be used as showing that "there is a way which seemeth right unto a man but the end thereof are the ways of death."

5. The last class of those who entertain false hopes, are those who say they are saved though they are leading sinful lives. In the case of many forms of sin, a good passage to use is 1 Cor. vi. 9–10. 1 John ii. 29 will also in many cases sweep away this false hope. 1 John v. 4–5 is useful as showing that one who is really born of God overcomes the world and the fact that they are living in sin and are not overcoming the world is evidence that they have not been born of God.

CHAPTER VII.

DEALING WITH THOSE WHO LACK ASSURANCE AND WITH BACK–SLIDERS

I. Those who Lack Assurance.

Those who lack assurance may be divided into two classes.

1. Those who lack assurance because of ignorance. 1 John v. 13, will show all such that we may know that we have eternal life. Often times when you ask people if they know they are saved, or if they know their sins are forgiven, or if they know they have eternal life, they will reply, "Why no one knows that." You can say to them, "Yes the Bible says that all who believe may know it," and then show them 1 John v. 13. John i. 12 shows that Christ gives to as many as receive Him, power to become the Sons of God. A good way to use this verse is to ask the inquirer questions regarding it. "What does every one who receives Him receive power to become?" The inquirer if he is attentively looking at the verse will answer, "A son of God." Then ask 58the next question, "Have you received Him?" If he replies "Yes," then ask him, "What are you then?" It will probably be necessary to go over it several times but at last the inquirer will see it and say "I am a son of God." John iii. 36 can be used in a similar way. Ask the inquirer "who do these verses say has everlasting life?" "He that believeth on the Son." "Do you believe on the Son?" "What have you then?" In a little while he will see it and say "Everlasting life." Then have him say over and over again "I have everlasting life," and have him kneel down and thank God for giving him everlasting life. One night I found a young man upon his knees at the close of the service in great distress. I showed him from the Bible

how Jesus Christ had borne his sins and asked him if he would accept Christ as his Saviour; he said he would; but he seemed to get no light and went out of the meeting in deep distress. The next night he was there again, professing to have accepted Christ but with no assurance that his sins were forgiven. I tried to show him from God's word what God said of those who accepted the Saviour, but the light did not come. Finally he rose to leave the meeting. I had just shown him from John iii. 36 that God said 59that "He that believeth on the Son hath everlasting life." As he turned to leave me, he said, "Will you pray for me?" I said "Yes." He walked a little way down the aisle and I called to him and said, "Do you believe I will pray for you?" He turned with a look of astonishment and replied, "Yes, of course." "Why do you think I will pray for you?" I then asked. "Because you said so," he replied. I said "Isn't God's word as good as mine?" He saw it at once, that while he had been willing to believe my word, he had not been willing to believe God's word, and he received assurance on the spot and knew that he had everlasting life. John v. 24 and 1 John v. 12 can be used in a similar way.

Acts xiii. 39 is very useful in dealing with this class of persons. Ask the inquirer: "What does this verse say that all who believe are?" "Justified." Then ask him, "Do you believe?" "What are you then?" It will probably take two or three times going over it before he sees it and when he answers "I am justified," tell him to thank God for justifying him and confess Christ, and see to it that he does so. Many inquirers of this class stumble over the fact that they have not the witness of the Holy Spirit. Show them from 601 John v. 10 that the witness of the word to their acceptance is sufficient, and that, if they believe not this witness of God in His word, they make Him a liar. Show them further from Eph. i. 13, that it is after we believe the testimony of the word that we are "sealed with the Holy Spirit of promise." The natural order in assurance is this: First, assurance of our justification, resting on the "Word of God." Second, public confession of Christ, "with the mouth," Romans x. 10. Third, the witness of the Holy Spirit. The trouble with many is that they wish to invert this order and have the witness of the Holy Spirit before they confess Christ with the mouth. From Matt. x. 32, 33, we learn that when we confess Christ before men, then He confesses us before the Father. We cannot reasonably expect the witness of the Spirit from the Father until we are confessed before the Father. So confession of Christ logically precedes the witness of the Spirit.

It is very important in using these texts to make clear what saving faith is; because many may say that they believe when they do not, in the sense of these texts, and so get a false assurance and entertain false hopes and never find deliverance. There is a great deal of careless 61dealing with those who lack assurance. Workers are so anxious to have inquirers come out clearly that they urge them on to assurance when they have no right to have assurance of salvation as they have not really accepted Christ.

John i. 12, and 2 Tim. i. 12, make very clear what believing is—receiving Jesus or committing to Jesus. Romans x. 10, will serve a similar purpose by showing that it "is with the heart man believeth unto righteousness."

2. Those who lack assurance because of sin. The trouble with those who lack assurance is, often, that there is some sin or questionable practice which they ought to confess and give up. John viii. 12; Is. lv. 7; Prov. xxviii. 13; Ps. xxxii. 1–5, are useful passages in dealing with this class of men, for they show that it is when sin is confessed and forsaken and we follow Christ, that we receive pardon, light and assurance. Often times it is well when one lacks assurance to put the question squarely to him: "Do you know of any sin on to which you are holding or anything in your life which your conscience troubles you about?"

II. Back–sliders. There are two classes of back–sliders and they should be dealt with in different ways.

621. Careless back–sliders; those who have no great desire to come back to the Saviour. With such persons use Jer. ii. 5, drive the question right home, "What iniquity have you found in the Lord?" Show them the base ingratitude and folly of forsaking such a Saviour and Friend. Very likely they have wandered away because of unkind treatment by professed Christians, but hold them right to the point of how the Lord treated them and how they are now treating Him. Use also Jer. ii. 13, and show them what they have forsaken and for what. Have them read the verse and ask them, "is not that verse true? When you forsook the Lord did you not forsake the 'fountain of living waters' and turn to 'broken cisterns that can hold no water?'" Illustrate the text by showing how foolish it would be to turn from a fountain of pure living water to broken cisterns or muddy pools. God has greatly honored this verse in bringing back–sliders back to himself. Use Jer. ii. 19. When they have read it ask them whether they have not found it "an evil thing and bitter" having forsaken the Lord their God. Prov. xiv. 14; 1 Kings xi. 9, and Luke xv. 13–17, can often times be used with effect with an impenitent back–slider, showing him 63the result of his wandering. I have a friend who always uses Amos. iv. 11, 12, and often times with good results.

2. Back–sliders who are sick of their wanderings and sin and desire to come back to the Lord. These are perhaps as easy a class to deal with as we ever find. Jer. iii. 12, 13, and 22, will show them how ready the Lord is to receive them back and that all he asks of them is that they acknowledge their sin and return to him. Hos. xiv. 1–4, is full of tender invitation to penitent back–sliders and also shows the way back to God. Is. xliii. 22, 24, 25, and Is. xliv. 20–22; Jer. xxix. 11–13; Deut. iv. 28–31; 2 Chron. vii. 14; 1 John i. 9; ii. 1–2, set forth God's unfailing love for the back–slider and His willingness to receive him back. Mark xvi. 7; 2 Chron. xv. 4;

xxxiii. 1–9, 12, 13, give illustrations of great back–sliders who returned to the Lord and how lovingly He received them, 1 John i. 9; Jer. iii. 12–13; 2 Chron. xv. 12, 15; vii. 14, show just what steps the back–slider must take to come back to the Lord and be restored to his favor, viz: humble himself, confess his sins and turn from his sin. Luke xv. 11–24, is perhaps the most useful passage of all in dealing with a back–slider who wishes to return for it has both 64the steps which the back–slider must take and the kind of reception he will receive.

When a back–slider has returned he should always be given instructions as to how to live so as not to back–slide again. The instruction to be given will be found in Chapter xii. sec. 15.

CHAPTER VIII.

DEALING WITH PROFESSED SKEPTICS AND INFIDELS

There are various classes of Sceptics and the same methods of dealing will not answer for all.

1. Skeptics who are mere triflers. With such use 1 Cor. i. 18. If a man says the Bible is foolishness to him, you can say "Yes, that is just what the Bible itself says." He will probably be surprised at this reply and then you can show him 1 Cor. i. 18; "the preaching of the cross is to them that perish foolishness." Then you can say to him, "You see that the Bible says that it is foolishness to some—them that perish—and the reason it is foolishness to you is because you are perishing." 1 Cor. ii. 14, can be used in a similar way. A worker was one night dealing with a man who said to him when he was trying to persuade him to come to Christ, "all that you are saying is foolishness to me." The worker quickly replied, "Yes, that is just what 66the Bible says." The man looked at him in astonishment and said: "What?" "You said all that I have been saying to you was foolishness to you, and that is just what the Bible says." The man was more astonished then than ever and the worker turned him to 1 Cor. ii. 14, "But the natural man receiveth not the things of the Spirit of God; for they are foolishness unto him; neither can he know them because they are spiritually discerned." The man said "I never saw that before; I never thought of it in that light before." 2 Cor. iv. 3, 4, is very useful in showing the trifler that he is lost and that his skepticism arises from the fact that the "god of this world hath blinded his mind." 2 Thes. ii. 10–12, is useful in showing the origin of skepticism, "because they received not the love of the truth"

and the consequences of skepticism—delusion and damnation. John viii. 21, 24, is also very searching in dealing with this class of skeptics, showing the terrible consequences of unbelief. John v. 44; iii. 18, 19, 20 expose the origin of scepticism. Ps. xiv. 1, is useful in some cases though one needs to be guarded in its use, using it only when it can be done with earnestness and tenderness. 2 Thes. i. 7, 8 can also be used with good results.

672. Serious minded skeptics. There is a large class of men and women in our day who are really desirous of knowing the truth but who are in an utter fog of skepticism. John vii. 17 is a very helpful passage in dealing with such. It shows the way out of skepticism to faith. Get the skeptic to act along the line of that verse. Put to him the question, "Will you surrender your will to God and promise to search honestly and earnestly to find out what God's will is that you may do it, to ask God to show you whether you need a Saviour and whether Jesus is a Divine Saviour, the Son of God; and will you promise that, if God will show you that Jesus is the Son of God, to accept Him as your Saviour and confess Him before the world?" Have him make his promise definite, by putting it down in black and white. If you get him to do this, his skepticism will soon take wings.

One evening at the close of a service I asked a gentleman why he was not a Christian. He replied: "I will tell you. I do not talk much about it; for I am not proud of it as some are, but I am a skeptic. I have lain awake nights thinking about this matter." "Do you believe there is a God?" "Yes, I never gave up my faith that there was 68a God." "Well, if there is a God you ought to obey him. Will you to–night take your stand upon the will of God to follow it wherever it carries you even if it carries you over the Niagara Falls?" "I try to do as near right as I know how." "That is not what I asked; will you take your stand on the will of God to follow it wherever it carries you?" "I have never put it that way." "Will you put it that way to–night?" "I will." "Do you believe God answers prayer?" "I don't know; I am afraid not." "You don't know that he does not?" "No." "Well, here is a possible clue to the truth, will you follow it, will you ask God to show you whether Jesus is His Son; and what your duty concerning him is?" "I will." Not long after that the man came into a meeting with a new look in his face. He arose and said: "I was all in a mist. I believed nothing." Then he told us what he had done. He had done just as he promised. "And now," he continued, "my doubts are all gone. I don't know where they have gone but they are gone." If the skeptic will not act in this way you can "stop his mouth" by showing him that he is not an honest skeptic and that the trouble with him is not his skepticism but his sin. If the man does not 69believe there is a God, you can begin one step further back. Ask him if he believes there is an absolute difference between right and wrong (if he does not he is a mere trifler). If he says he does, ask him if he will take his stand upon the right and follow it wherever it carries him. He may try to put you off by saying "What is right?" or that he is doing the right as nearly as he knows how. Get him to promise that he will take his stand upon the right, whatever he may find it to be and follow it whatever the consequence may be. Then show him that if he is honest in this promise, he will try to find out what the right is. Next say to him, "You do not know whether God answers prayer or not. I know He does, and you will admit that here is a possible clue to knowledge. If you are honest in your desire to know the truth, you will follow this possible clue. You can get down and at least pray, 'O my God, if there be a God, teach me thy will and I will do it. Show me whether Jesus is thy son or not. If you show that he is, I will accept Him as my Saviour and confess Him before the world.'" Then tell the man to begin reading the Gospel of John, reading slowly and thoughtfully, only a few verses at 70a time, asking God for light each time before reading and promising God that he will follow the light as fast as He makes it clear. If the man will follow this rational course, it will result in every case in the skeptic coming out into the clear light of faith in the Bible, as the word of God, and Jesus Christ as the Son of God. If the man is not an honest skeptic, this course of treatment will reveal the fact and then you can show him that the difficulty is not with his skepticism but with his rebellious heart.

If the man says that he does not know whether there is an absolute difference between right and wrong, then you can set it down at once that he is bad and turn upon him kindly and earnestly and say to him, "My friend, there is something wrong in your life; no man that is living right doubts that there is a difference between right and wrong. Now you probably know what is wrong and the trouble is not with your skepticism, but with your sin." One afternoon after I had given out an invitation for any skeptic or any one else who wished to talk with me, to remain after the meeting, a young man with whom I had dealt some months before stayed. I asked him what his trouble was. 71He replied, "The same trouble that I told you in the spring, I cannot believe that there is a God." I asked him if he had done as I had advised him to do in our former conversation; if he had taken his stand upon the right to follow it wherever it carried him. He replied that he did not know that there was any difference between right and wrong. "I do not know that there is such a thing as right." I looked him right in the eyes and said, "Is there some sin your life?"

He said "Yes." I said "what is it?" He replied, "The same that I told you last spring." I said, "You promised to give it up, have you given it up?" He said "No, I have not." "Well," I said, "there is the difficulty, not with your skepticism. Give up that sin and your skepticism will take care of itself." In some confusion he replied, "I guess that is the trouble."

3. Those who doubt the existence of God.

The passages under 1 and 2 can also be used with this class and generally it is wise to use them before those given under this head. There are however, three passages that are often times effective with this specific class of skeptics. Ps. xiv. 1; before using this passage you can say to the man, "Let me read you from God's own word what he 72says about those who deny his existence." Often times it is well to leave the passage to do its own work. Sometimes, however, it is wise to dwell a little upon it. Call the man's attention to the fact that it is "in his heart" that the fool says "there is no God." He does not believe there is a God because he does not wish to. You can add that the folly of saying in one's heart that there is no God is seen in two points; first, there is a God and it is folly to say there is not one, and second, the doctrine that there is not a God always brings misery and wretchedness. Put it right to the man, and ask him if he ever knew a happy atheist. Ps. xix. 1, 2; Romans i. 19–22, are also effective passages.

4. Those who doubt that the Bible is the word of God.

Romans iii. 3, 4, is useful in showing that questioning the fact does not alter the fact. Matt. xxiv. 35, is often used by the Spirit to carry to the heart of the skeptic the certainty and immutability of God's word. Mark vii. 13; Matt. v. 18; John x. 35; Luke xxiv. 27, 44, are useful as giving Christ's testimony that the Old Testament is the Word of God. They are especially helpful in dealing with those who say that they accept the authority of 73Christ but not that of the Old Testament, for in them Christ sets His seal to the Old Testament Scriptures and they show conclusively that if we accept His authority we must accept that of the Old Testament also. Along the same line John xiv. 26, and xvi. 12, 13, are useful as containing Christ's indorsement of the New Testament.

1 Thes. ii. 13, can be used with good effect to meet the statement which is often made, that Paul nowhere claims that his teaching is the word of God. 2 Peter i. 21, John viii. 47; Luke xvi. 30, 31, can also be used in dealing with this class. 2 John v. 10, is very effective in showing the guilt of

those who believe not the record that God has given. Before using this last passage you can say, "You doubt, do you, that the Bible is the Word of God? Now let us see what God says about those that believe not His testimony;" then turn them to the passage and have them read it.

5. Those who doubt a future existence.

1 Cor. xv. 35–36; Jno. v. 28–29; Dan. xii. 2.

6. Those who doubt the doctrine of future punishment, or the conscious, endless suffering of the lost. Rev. xxi. 8, defines what "death" means when used in the scriptures 74Rev. xvii. 8, compared with Rev. xix. 20, shows what perdition or destruction means in the scriptures. Rev. xix. 20, compared with Rev. xx. 10 shows that "the lake of fire" is not a place where those consigned to it cease to exist, for we find in the latter passage the beast and false prophet are still there at the end of a thousand years and that they, so far from being annihilated or losing conscious existence are tormented night and day forever and ever. Rev. xiii. 7–8 show that those who are subjected to the terrible retribution here described are those whose names are not written in the Book of Life. Matt. x. 28 shows that there is destruction for the soul apart from the destruction of the body. Luke xii. 5, shows that after one is killed and is of course dead, there is a punishment in "hell." Mark iii. 28–29 (R. V.) shows that there is such a thing as eternal sin. Luke xvi. 23–26, shows that the condition of the wicked dead is one of conscious torment. Mark xiv. 21, shows that the retribution visited upon the wicked is of so stern a character that it would be better for him upon whom it is visited if he had never been born.

2 Peter ii. 4; Jude 6, show that hell is not a place where the inhabitants cease to 75exist, but where they are reserved alive, for the purpose of God. Heb. x. 28–29, show that while the punishment of transgression of the Mosaic law was death, that sorer punishment awaits those who have

"trodden under foot the Son of God." Matt. xxv. 41 gives further light upon the subject. It shows that the wicked go to the same place with the Beast and False Prophet and the Devil mentioned in Rev. xix. 20, and xx. 10, and share the same endless, conscious torment.

7. Those who doubt the divinity of Christ.

a. In Acts x. 36; 1 Cor. ii. 8, compare Ps. xxiv. 8–10; Heb. i. 8; John xx. 28; Rom. ix. 5; Rev. i. 17, compare Is. xliv. 6, we find several divine titles applied to Christ, the same titles being applied to Christ in the New Testament that are applied to Jehovah in the old.

b. In Heb. i. 10, 3, we find divine offices attributed to Christ.

c. In John v. 22–23, compare Rev. v. 13; Heb. i. 6; Phil. ii. 10, we find it taught that Jesus Christ should be worshiped as God.

d. In John v. 22–23 we find Jesus claiming the same honor as his Father, and either He was Divine or the most blasphemous impostor that ever lived. Drive it home that the 76one who denies Christ's Divinity puts Him in the place of a blasphemous imposter. Mark xiv. 61, 62, can be used in a similar way.

e. 1 Jno. ii. 22, 23, compared with 1 Jno. v. 1, 5, shows that the one who denies the Divinity of Christ, no matter who he may be, is a liar and an antichrist. 1 Jno. v. 10–12, shows that he who does not believe that Jesus is divine makes God a liar, "Because he believeth not the record that God gave of His Son." Heb. x. 28–29, shows the folly, guilt and punishment of rejecting Christ as the Son of God. John viii. 24, shows beyond a question that no one who does not believe in the Divinity of Jesus Christ will be saved. Jno. xx. 31, shows that we have life through believing that Jesus is the Christ, the son of God.

(Note. It is best as a rule before taking up specific difficulties to deal with the inquirer with the passage under the head of "Skeptics who are triflers," or those under "Serious minded skeptics.")

Often times there is no need to take up specific questions as for example about future punishment until the inquirer has first settled the matter whether he will accept Christ as his Saviour.

CHAPTER IX.

DEALING WITH THE COMPLAINING

1. Those who complain of God.

Many that you wish to lead to Christ will say something to the effect that God is unjust and cruel, Job. xl. 2, and Romans ix. 20, are very pointed passages to use with inquirers of this class and need no comment. It might be well to preface the reading of the passages with some remark like this; "Do you know of how enormous a sin you are guilty in accusing God of being unjust and cruel? Let me read what God says about it in His Word." Then read the passages. Romans xi. 33 will serve to show the complaining that the reason God's ways seem unjust and cruel is because they are so deep and unsearchable; and that the trouble is not with God's ways but the limitation of their understanding. Heb. xii. 5, 7, 10, 11 are especially useful in cases where the inquirer complains because of his own misfortunes or sorrows. Is. lv. 8–9 will often times prove helpful. Not infrequently 78you will meet with one who will say that "God is unjust to create men and then damn them." Turn such an one to Ezek. xxxiii. 11. This passage meets this complaint by showing that God has no pleasure in the death of the wicked, but desires their welfare and that the wicked bring damnation upon themselves by their stubborn refusal to repent. 1 Tim. ii. 3–4, shows that God, so far from creating man to damn him, desires that all men be saved. 2 Peter iii. 9, teaches that God is not willing that any should perish and is delaying His purposes in order that all may come to repentance. John v. 40, and Matt. xxiii. 37, show that the whole cause of man's damnation is his own willful and persistent refusal to come to Christ. John iii. 36, and iii. 16, are also helpful in many cases.

2. Those who complain of the bible. Men will often times say, "The Bible is contradictory and absurd;" or "the Bible seems foolish to me." Two classes of passages can be used in dealing with such inquirers.

a. 1 Cor. i. 18; ii. 14; 2 Cor. iv. 3–4; Dan. xii. 10; Rom. xi. 33, 34 and in extreme cases 2 Thes. ii. 10, 11, 12.

b. Jno. vii. 17; Ps. xxv. 14; Matt. xi. 25, (see remarks under Serious Minded Skeptics 79and Skeptics who are Triflers.) Sometimes the best thing to do with a man who says the Bible is full of contradictions, is to hand him your Bible and ask him to show you one. In most cases he will not attempt to do it; as people who complain about the Bible, as a rule know nothing about its contents. One day a man was brought to me to deal with and when I asked him why he was not a Christian he replied, "The Bible is full of contradictions." I at once asked him to show me one. "Oh!" he said, "it's full of them." I said, "If it is full of them you ought to be able to show me one." He said, "Well, there is one in Psalms." I said, "Show it to me." He commenced looking in the back of the New Testament for the book of Psalms. I said, "You are not looking in the right part of the Bible for Psalms. Let me find it for you." I found him the book of Psalms and handed it to him. After fumbling around he said, "I could find it, if I had my own Bible here." "Well," I said, "Will you bring your Bible to–night?" He promised he would and agreed to meet me at a certain place in the church. The appointed hour came, but he did not. Some months afterwards in another series of meetings in the same church one of the workers stopped 80me and said, "Here's a man I wish you would deal with; he is a skeptic." I looked at him and recognized him as the same man. "Oh!" I said, "you are the man that lied to me here;" and with much confusion he admitted that he was, but he was still playing his old game of saying that the Bible was full of contradictions. In nine cases out of ten, men who say this, know nothing about the Bible, and when you ask them to show you a contradiction in the Bible they are filled with confusion.

3. Those who complain of God's way of Salvation.

A great many men will say, "I do not see why God could not save men in some other way than by the death of His son." Is. lv. 8, 9, Romans xi. 33 are useful in dealing with such. I have used Romans ix. 20 with effect with men of this sort. A young student said to me one night, when I asked why he was not a Christian, that he did not see why it was necessary for Christ to die for him; why God did not save him in some other way. I opened my Bible and read to him Romans ix. 20, and put the question right to him, "Who art thou that repliest against God?" and then said to him, "Do you realize what you are 81doing, that you are condemning God?" The young man very much confused said "I did not mean to do that." "Well," I said; "that is what you are doing." "If that is so," he replied, "I will take it back." A good way to do with such men is to show them by the use of passages given under the chapter "Dealing with the Indifferent" that they are lost sinners. When any one is led to see this, God's way of salvation will approve itself as just the thing.

4. Those who complain of Christians. Very frequently when we try to persuade men to accept Christ as their Saviour, they reply; "There are too many hypocrites in church." Romans xiv. 4 and 12, especially the latter verse, are exceedingly effective in dealing with such.

Romans ii. 1, and Matt. vii. 1–5, are also excellent. Jno. xxi. 21, 22 is useful in showing the objector that he is solely responsible for his own relation to Christ and that what others do is none of his affairs. Sometimes the inquirer will complain of the way Christian people have treated him. In such a case turn the attention of the inquirer from the way in which Christian people have treated him to the way in which God has treated him. For 82this purpose use Jer. ii. 5; Is. liii. 5; Romans v. 6–8. Then ask him if the fact that Christians have treated him badly is any excuse for his treatment of a Heavenly Father who has treated him so well. One night turning to an aged man I asked him if he was a Christian. He replied that he was not, that he was a back–slider. I asked him why he back–slid. He replied that Christian people had treated him badly. I opened my Bible and read Jer. ii. 5, to him, "Thus saith the Lord, what iniquity have your fathers found in me, that they are gone far from me, and have walked after vanity and are become vain?" I said, "Did you find any iniquity in God? Did God not use you well?" With a good deal of feeling the man admitted that God had not treated him badly and I held him right to this point of God's treatment of him, and not man's treatment, and his treatment of God. Matt. xviii. 23–35; Eph. iv. 30–32; Matt. vi. 14–15, are also useful as showing the absolute necessity of our forgiving men.

CHAPTER X.

DEALING WITH THOSE WHO WISH TO PUT OFF A DECISION UNTIL SOME OTHER TIME

1. There are several classes of those who wish to put off a decision. One of the largest is composed of those who say "I want to wait," or "Not to–night," or "I will think about it," or "I will come to–morrow night," or some such thing. Use Is. lv. 6. The inquirer having read the passage, ask him when it is that he is to seek the Lord, and when he answers "While he may be found," ask him when that is and then drive it home. Ask him if he is sure that he can find Him to–morrow if he does not seek Him to–day. Or you can use Prov. xxix. 1. It is well after he has read this verse to ask the one with whom you are dealing what becomes of the one who "being often reproved hardeneth his neck" and when he answers "He shall be destroyed," ask him how he shall be destroyed, and when he answers "Suddenly," ask him if he is willing to run the risk. Or you can use Matt. xxv. 10–12. 84Ask him who it was that went into the marriage? and when he answers "They that were ready" ask him if he is ready. Then ask him what happened after those who were ready went in. Then ask him where "those who were not ready" were. Then put it to him, "Are you willing to be on the out–side?" Or you can use Luke xii. 19, 20. Ask the inquirer for how long a time this man thought he had made provision. Then ask him: "If God should call you to–night would you be ready?" Matt. xxiv. 44, is especially effective in dealing with those who say "I am not ready." 1 Kings xviii. 21, can be used with good effect. An excellent way to use this verse is by asking the person whether he would be willing to wait a year and not

have an opportunity under any circumstances, no matter what came up, of accepting Christ. When he answers, "No, I might die within a year," ask him if he would be willing to wait a month. Then bring it down to a week and finally to a day, and ask him if he would like God and the Holy Spirit and all Christians to leave him alone for a day and he not have an opportunity, under any circumstances of accepting Christ? Almost any thoughtful person will say, "No." Then tell him that if that is the case he had better 85accept Christ at once. Dr. Chalmers was the first one to use this method and it has been followed by many others with great success. Prov. xxvii. 1; James iv. 13, 14; Job. xxxvi. 18; Luke xiii. 24–28; xii. 19, 20; John viii. 21; xii. 35; vii. 33–34, can also be used with this class.

2. Those who say "I must get fixed in business first, then I will become a Christian," or "I must do something else first." Matt. vi. 33, is the great passage to use in such cases; for it shows that we must seek the kingdom of God first.

3. Those who say "I am waiting God's time." If one says this, ask him if he will accept Christ in God's time if you will show him when God's time is. Then turn to 2 Cor. vi. 2, or Heb. iii. 15.

4. Those who say "I am too young," or "I want to wait until I am older." Ecc. xii. 1, is an all–sufficient answer to such. Matt. xix. 14, and xviii. 3, are also good passages to use as they show that youth is the best time to come to Christ and that all must become children, even if they are old, before they can enter into the kingdom of Heaven. It is often times wise in dealing with persons who wish to put off a decision until some time in the future to use the passages given for "The Indifferent," 86until such a deep impression is made of their need of Christ that they will not be willing to postpone accepting Christ.

In dealing with those under "1" above, it is best to use only one passage and drive that home by constant repetition. One night I was dealing with a man who was quite interested but who kept saying "I cannot decide to–night." I quoted Prov. xxix. 1. To every answer he made I would come back to this passage. I must have repeated it a great many times in the course of the talk until the man was made to feel not only his need of Christ but the danger of delaying and the necessity of a prompt decision. He tried to get away from the passage but I held him to this one point. The passage lingered with him and it was emphasized by the providence of God; for that very night he was assaulted and quite seriously injured, and he came the next night with his head bandaged and accepted Christ. The pounding which he received from his assailant would probably have done him little good if the text of scripture had not been pounded into his mind.

87

CHAPTER XI.

DEALING WITH THE WILLFUL AND THE DELUDED

1. The Willful

There are several varieties of the Willful. There are those for example who say "I do not wish you to talk to me." In such a case it is usually best to give some pointed passage of scripture and let it talk for itself and then leave the person alone to reflect upon it. Romans vi. 23; Heb. x. 28, 29; Heb. xii. 25; Mark xvi. 16; Prov. xxix. 1, and Prov. i. 24–33, are passages which are good for this purpose.

Then there are those who say "I cannot forgive." Matt. vi. 15 and xviii. 23–35, are good to use as showing that they must forgive or be lost. Phil. iv. 13, and Ezek. xxxvi. 26, will show them how they can forgive. There are a great many people who are kept from Christ by an unforgiving spirit. Some times this difficulty can be removed by getting 88the person to kneel in prayer and ask God to take away their unforgiving spirit. I once reasoned a long time with an inquirer who was under deep conviction, but was held back from accepting Christ by a hatred in her heart toward some one who had wronged her. She kept insisting that she could not forgive. Finally I said, "let us get down and tell God about this matter." To this she consented and scarcely had we knelt when she burst into a flood of tears, and the difficulty was removed and she accepted Christ immediately.

There are those again who say "I love the world too much." Mark viii. 36, is the great text to use with this class. Luke xiv. 33, will show the absolute necessity that the world be given up. Luke xii. 16–20; 1 Jno. ii. 15, 16, 17, will show the folly of holding on to the world and Ps. lxxxiv. 11, Romans viii. 32, will show that the Lord will hold back no good thing from them.

There are those who say “I cannot acknowledge a wrong that I have done.” Prov. xxviii. 13, will show the wretchedness and woe that is sure to follow unless the wrong is acknowledged. Others will say “I do not want to make a public confession.” Romans x. 10; Matt. x. 32, 33, will show that God will accept nothing 89else. Mark viii. 38; Jno. xii. 42, 43, and Prov. xxix. 25, will show the peril of not making it. There are those who say “I want to have my own way.” Is. lv. 8–9, will show how much better God’s way is, and Prov. xiv. 12, shows the consequences of having our own way. Finally there are those who say “I neither accept Christ nor reject Him.” Matt. xii. 30, will show that they must do one or the other. This verse has been used to the conviction of a great many.

2. The Deluded

a. Under this head come the Roman Catholics. A good way to deal with a Roman Catholic is to show him the necessity of the new birth and what the new birth is. Jno. iii. 3, 5, 7, shows the necessity of the new birth. What the new birth is, is shown in Ezek. xxxvi. 25–27; 2 Cor. v. 17; 2 Peter i. 4. Many Roman Catholics understand the new birth to mean baptism, but it can be easily shown them that the language used does not fit baptism. Further than this, in 1 Cor. iv. 15, Paul says to the Corinthian Christians he had begotten them again through the gospel. If the new birth meant baptism he must have baptized them, but in 1 Cor. i. 14, he declares he had not baptized them. Acts 90viii. 13, 21, 23, shows that a man may be baptized, and yet his heart not be “right in the sight of God” so he has “neither part nor lot in this matter.” It is well to take a step further and show the inquirer what the evidences of the new birth are. 1 Jno. ii.

29; iii. 9, 14–17; v. 1, 4, give the Biblical evidences of the new birth. The next question that will arise is "How to be born again." This question is answered in Jno. i. 12; 1 Peter i. 23; Jas. i. 18.

Acts iii. 19, is a good text to use with Roman Catholics as it shows the necessity of repentance and conversion. What repentance is, will be shown by Is. lv. 7; Jonah iii. 10. Still another way of dealing with Roman Catholics is by showing them that it is the believer's privilege to know that he has eternal life. Roman Catholics almost always lack assurance. They do not know that they are forgiven, but hope to be forgiven some day. If you can show them that we may know that we are forgiven and that we have eternal life, it will awaken in a great many of them a desire for this assurance. 1 John v. 13, shows that it is the believer's privilege to know. Acts xiii. 38, 39; x. 43, John iii. 36, are very useful in leading them into this assurance. Still another way 91of dealing with them (but it is not best to use it until you have already made some progress with them) is to show them the advantage of Bible study. Good texts for this purpose are John v. 39; 1 Peter ii. 1, 2; 2 Tim. iii. 13–17; Jas i. 21, 22; Ps. i. 1, 2; Josh. i. 8; Mark vii. 7, 8, 13; Matt. xxii. 29. These texts, excepting the one in 1 Peter ii. 1, 2, are all practically the same in the "Douay" or Roman Catholic Bible as they are in the Protestant Bible and it is well oftentimes in dealing with a Catholic to use the Catholic Bible.

Still another way of dealing with a Roman Catholic is to use the same method that you would in dealing with an impenitent sinner—that is to awaken a sense that he is a sinner and needs Christ. For this purpose use Matt. xxii. 37, 38; Gal. iii. 10, 13; Is. liii. 6.

Many people think that there is no use of talking with Roman Catholics, that they cannot be brought to Christ. This is a great mistake. Many of them are longing for something they do not find in the Roman Catholic church, and, if you can show them from the word of God how to find it, they come along very easily and they make very earnest Christians. Do not attack the Roman Catholic church. Give them the truth, and the errors 92in time will take care of themselves. Often times our attacks only expose our ignorance.

There is one point at which we always have the advantage in dealing with a Roman Catholic; that is that there is peace and power in Christianity as we know it that there is not in Christianity as they know it, and they appreciate the difference.

b. Jews. The best way to deal with a Jew is to show him that his own Bible points to Christ. The most helpful passages to use are Is. liii.; Dan. ix. 26; Zech. xii. 10. There are also useful passages in the New Testament; the whole book of Hebrews, especially the ninth and tenth chapters and the seventh chapter, 25th to 28th verses, and the whole Gospel of Matthew. A great many Jews to–day are inquiring into the claims of Jesus of Nazareth, and are open to approach upon this subject. The great difficulty in the way of the Jew coming out as a Christian is the terrific persecution which he must endure if he does. This difficulty can be met by the passages already given under the head of "Those Who are Afraid of Persecution."

(Note. There are a number of good tracts for Jews which can be had from the Mildmay 93Mission to the Jews, 79 Mildmay Road, London.)

c. Spiritualists. Lev. xix. 31; xx. 6; Deut. xviii. 10–12; 2 Kings xxi. 1, 2, 6; 1 Chron. x. 13; Is. viii. 19, 20; 1 John iv. 1–3; 2 Thes. ii. 9–12, are passages to be used with this class.

In dealing with all classes of deluded people it is well to begin by using Jno. vii. 17, and bring them to a place where they heartily desire to know the truth. There is no hope of bringing a man out of his delusion, unless he desires to know the truth.

CHAPTER XII.

SOME HINTS AND SUGGESTIONS

There are a few general suggestions to be made that will prove helpful to the worker.

1. As a rule choose persons to deal with of your own sex and about your own age. There are exceptions to this rule. One should be always looking to the Holy Spirit for his guidance as to whom to approach, and He may lead us to one of the opposite sex, but unless there is clear guidance in the matter, it is quite commonly agreed among those who have had large experience in Christian work that men do, on the whole, most satisfactory work with men, and women with women. Especially is this true of the young. Many unfortunate complications oftentimes arise when young men try to lead young women to Christ or vice versa. Of course, an elderly motherly woman may do excellent work with a young man or boy, and an elderly, fatherly man may do good work with a young woman or girl. It is not 95wise ordinarily for a young and inexperienced person to approach one very much older and maturer and wiser than themselves on this subject.

2. Whenever it is possible, get the person with whom you are dealing alone. No one likes to open his heart freely to another on this most personal and sacred of all subjects when there are others present. Many will from pride defend themselves in a false position when several are present, who would fully admit their error or sin or need, if they were alone with you. As a rule it is far better for a single worker to deal with a single unconverted person, than for several workers to

deal with a single inquirer or for a single worker to deal with several inquirers at once. If you have several to deal with take them one by one. Workers often find that when they have made no headway while talking to several at once, by taking individuals off by themselves they soon succeed in leading them one by one to Christ.

3. Let your reliance be wholly in the Spirit of God and the Word of God.

4. Do not content yourself with merely reading passages from the Bible—much less in merely quoting them, but have the one with 96whom you are dealing read them himself that the truth may find entrance into the heart through the eye as well as the ear.

5. It is ofttimes well to use but a single passage of scripture, drive that home and clinch it so that the one with whom you have been dealing cannot forget it, but will hear it ringing in his memory long after you have ceased talking. Dr. Ichabod Spencer once in dealing with a young man who had many difficulties kept continually quoting the passage "now is the accepted time, behold now is the day of salvation." The young man tried to get Dr. Spencer on to something else, but over and over again he rang out the words. The next day the young man returned rejoicing in Christ and thanking the doctor that he had "hammered" him with that text. The words kept ringing in his ears during the night and he could not rest until he had settled the matter by accepting Christ. It is a good thing when a person can point to some definite verse in the word of God and say "I know on the authority of that verse that my sins are forgiven and I am a child of God." There are times, however when a powerful effect is produced by a piling up of passages along some line until the mind is convinced and the heart conquered.

976. Always hold the person with whom you are dealing to the main point of accepting Christ. If he wishes to discuss

the claims of various denominations, or the question of baptism, or theories of future punishment or any other question other than the central one of his need of a Saviour and Christ the Saviour he needs; tell him that those questions are proper to take up in their right place and time, but the time to settle them is after he has settled the first and fundamental question of accepting or rejecting Christ. Many a case has been lost by an inexperienced worker allowing himself to be involved in a discussion of some side issue which it is utter folly to discuss with an unregenerated person.

7. Be courteous. Many well–meaning but indiscreet Christians by their rudeness and impertinence repel those whom they would win to Christ. It is quite possible to be at once perfectly frank and perfectly courteous. You can point out to men their awful sin and need without insulting them. Your words may be very searching, while your manner is very gentle and winning. Indeed, the more gentle and winning our manner is, the deeper our words will go, for they will not stir up the opposition of those with whom we deal. 98Some zealous workers approach those with whom they wish to deal in such a manner that the latter at once assume the defensive and clothe themselves with an armor that it is impossible to penetrate.

8. Be dead in earnest. Only the earnest man can make the unsaved man feel the truth of God's word. It is well to let the passages that we would use with others first sink into our own souls. I know of a very successful worker who for a long time used the one passage, "prepare to meet thy God," with every one with whom she dealt, but that passage had taken such complete possession of her heart and mind that she used it with tremendous effect. A few passages that have mastered us are better than many passages that we have mastered from some text book.

The reader of this book is advised to ponder, upon his knees, such of the passages suggested in it as he decides to use until he himself feels their power. We read of Paul that he “ceased not to warn every one night and day, with tears.” (Acts xx. 31.) Genuine earnestness will go farther than any skill learned in a training class or from the study of such a book as this.

9. Never lose your temper when trying to 99lead a soul to Christ. Some persons are purposely exasperating, but even such may be won, by patience, forbearance and gentleness.

They certainly cannot be won if you lose your temper. Nothing delights them more, or gives them more comfort in their sins. The more extremely irritating they are in their words and actions the more impressed they will be if you return insults with kindness. Often times the one who has been most insufferable will come back in penitence. One of the most insulting men I ever met afterwards became one of the most patient, persistent and effective of workers.

10. Never have a heated argument with one whom you would lead to Christ. This always comes from the flesh and not from the spirit. (Gal. v. 20, 22, 23.) It arises from pride and unwillingness to let the other person get the best of you in argument. Refuse to argue. If the one with whom you are talking has mistaken notions that must be removed before he can be led to Christ quietly and pleasantly show him their error. If the error is not essential refuse to discuss it and hold the person to the main question.

11. Never interrupt any one else who is dealing with a soul. You may think he is 100not doing it in the wisest way, but if you can do it any better, bide your time and you will have the opportunity. Many an unskilled worker has had some one at the very point of decision when some meddler has broken in and upset the whole work. On the other hand,

do not let others, if you can help it, interrupt you. Just a little word plainly but courteously spoken will usually prevent it.

12. Don't be in a hurry. One of the great faults of Christian work to–day is haste. We are too anxious for immediate results and so do superficial work. It is very noticeable how many of those with whom Christ dealt came out slowly. Nicodemus, Joseph, Peter and even Paul—though the final step in his case seems very sudden—are cases in point. It was three days even after the personal appearance of Jesus to Paul on the way to Damascus before the latter came out into the light and openly confessed Christ. (Acts xxii. 16.) One man with whom slow but thorough work has been done, and who at last has been brought out clearly for Christ, is better than a dozen with whom hasty work has been done, who think they have accepted Christ when in reality they have not. It is often a wise policy to plant a truth in a man's heart and 101leave it to work. The seed on rocky ground springs up quickly but withers as quickly.

13. Whenever it is possible and wise, get the person with whom you are dealing on his knees before God. It is wonderful how many difficulties disappear in prayer, and how readily stubborn people yield when they are brought into the very presence of God himself. I remember talking with a young woman, in an inquiry room, for perhaps two hours and making no apparent headway; but, when at last we knelt in prayer, in less than five minutes she was rejoicing in her Saviour.

14. Whenever you seem to fail in any given case go home and pray over it and study it to see why you failed. If you have been at a loss as to what scripture to use, study that portion of this book that describes the different classes we meet and how to deal with them and see where this case belongs and how you ought to have treated it. Then go back if you can and try again. In any case you will be better

prepared next time. The greatest success in this work comes through many apparent defeats. It will be well to frequently study these hints and suggestions to see if your failures come through neglect of them.

15. Before parting from the one who has 102accepted Christ, be sure to give him definite instructions as to how to succeed in the Christian life. The following are points that should be always insisted upon. (a.) Confess Christ with the mouth before men every opportunity you get. Rom. x. 9, 10; Matt. x. 32, 33. (b.) Be baptized and partake regularly of the Lord's supper. Acts ii. 38, 42; Luke xxii. 19; 1 Cor. xi. 24–26. (c.) Study the Word of God daily. 1 Pet. ii. 2; Acts xx. 32; 2 Tim. iii. 13–17; Acts xvii. 11. (d.) Pray daily, often and in every time of temptation. Luke xi. 9–13; xxii. 40; 1 Thes. v. 17. (e.) Put away out of your life every sin, even the smallest, and everything you have doubts about, and obey every word of Christ 1 Jno. i. 6, 7; Rom. xiv. 23; Jno. xiv. 23. (f.) Seek the society of Christians. Eph. iv. 12–16; Acts ii. 42, 47; Heb. x. 24, 25. (g.) Go to work for Christ. Matt. xxv. 14–29. (h.) When you fall into sin don't be discouraged, but confess it at once, believe it is forgiven because God says so and get up and go on. 1 Jno. i. 9; Phil. iii. 13–14. It would be well to give these instructions in some permanent form to the one whom you have led to Christ. You can write them out or get a little tract called the "Christian Life Card" published by Jno. C. Collins, 103Bureau of Supplies, New Haven, Conn. This contains them and some other matter.

16. When you have led any one to Christ, follow him up and help him in the development of his Christian life. Many are led to Christ and then neglected and get on very poorly. This is a great mistake. The work of following up those who are converted is as important as the work of leading them to Christ, and as a rule no one can do it so well as the person whom God used in their conversion.

CHAPTER XIII.

THE BAPTISM OF THE HOLY SPIRIT

There is one condition of success in bringing men to Christ that is of such cardinal importance, and so little understood, that it demands a separate chapter. I refer to the Baptism of the Holy Spirit. In Acts i. 5; Luke xxiv. 49 (comp. Acts i. 8), and Acts ii. 4, we have three expressions; "baptized with the Holy Spirit," "endured with power from on high" and "filled with the Holy Spirit." By a careful comparison of these and related passages we will find that these various expressions refer to one and the same experience. This experience we shall see as we proceed in the study of this subject is an absolutely necessary condition of acceptable and effective service for Christ.

1. What is the Baptism of the Holy Spirit?

1. It is a definite and distinct operation of the Holy Spirit of which one may know whether it has been wrought in him or not. 105This is evident from the fact that Jesus bade His disciples tarry in Jerusalem until they had received this enduement, (Luke xxiv. 49, comp. Acts i. 8), and if it was not a definite and distinct operation of which they might know whether they had received it or not, of course, they would not know when this command of Christ had been complied with and when they were ready to begin their witnessing.

2. It is an operation of The Holy Spirit separate from His regenerating work. This appears from Acts i. 5, where the disciples are told "ye shall be baptized with the Holy Spirit not many days hence." But from Jno. xv. 3; xiii. 10 we learn

that the disciples were already regenerated. It appears also from Acts viii. 15, 16 where we are told of certain who had already believed and were baptized with water, but upon whom the Holy Spirit had not yet fallen. The same thing is shown by Acts xix. 1–6, where we are told of certain who were disciples, but who had not received the Holy Spirit since they believed. One may then be regenerated by the Holy Spirit without being baptized with the Holy Spirit. Such an one is saved but he is not yet fitted for service. Every believer has the Holy Spirit, Rom. viii. 1069, but not every believer has the Baptism of the Holy Spirit, (Acts viii. 12–16; xix. 1–2). We shall see very soon that every believer may have the baptism of the Holy Spirit.

3. The Baptism of the Holy Spirit is always connected with testimony or service, (see 1 Cor. xii. 4–13; Acts i. 5–8; Luke xxiv. 49; Acts ii. 4; iv. 8, 31; vii. 55; ix. 17, 20; x. 45–46; xix. 6.) The Baptism of the Holy Spirit has no direct reference to cleansing from sin. This is an important point to bear in mind for many reasons. There is a line of teaching on this subject that leads men to expect that if they receive the Baptism of the Holy Spirit, the old carnal nature will be eradicated. There is not a line of scripture to support this position. As said above, and as any one can learn for himself if he will examine all the passages in which the baptism of the Holy Spirit is mentioned, it is always connected with testimony and service. It is indeed accompanied with a great moral and spiritual uplifting and pre–supposes, as we shall see, an entire surrender of the will to Christ, but its primary and immediate purpose is fitting for service. We will get a more definite idea of what the Baptism of the Holy Spirit is, if we consider its manifestations and results as stated in the 107Bible. (a.) Let us look first at the passage that goes most into detail on this subject, 1 Cor. xii. 4–13. We see at once that the manifestations or results of the Baptism of the Holy Spirit are not precisely the same in all persons. For example, the Baptism of the Holy Spirit will not make every one who receives it a successful evangelist or teacher. Some quite

different gift may be imparted. This fact is often overlooked and much disappointment and doubt are the result. The manifestations or results vary with the lines of service to which God has called different individuals. One receives the gift of an evangelist, another of a teacher, another of government, another of a helper, another of a mother, (1 Cor. xii. 28–31; Eph. iv. 8, 11.) (b.) 1 Cor. xii. 7, 11. There will be some gift in every case. Not the same gift but some gift, of an evangelist, or a pastor, or of a teacher or some other. (c.) 1 Cor. xii. 11. The Holy Spirit is Himself the one who decides what the gift or gifts shall be which he will impart to each individual. It is not for us to select some place of service and then ask the Holy Spirit to qualify us for that service, nor for us to select some gift, and then ask the Spirit to impart to us that gift. It is for us to put ourselves 108entirely at the disposal of the Holy Spirit to send us where "He will," into what line of service "He will" (Acts xiii. 2,) and to impart what gift "He will." He is absolutely sovereign and our rightful position is that of absolute and unconditional surrender to Him. This is where many fail of a blessing and meet with disappointment. I know a most sincere and self–sacrificing man who gave up a lucrative business and took up the work of an evangelist. He had heard of the Baptism of the Holy Spirit; and had been led to suppose that, if he received it, it would qualify him for the work of an evangelist. The man came more than four thousand miles to this country, but the work did not open to him. He was in much perplexity and doubt until he was led to see that it was not for him to select the work of an evangelist, as good as that work was, and then expect the Holy Spirit to qualify him for this self–chosen work. He gave himself up to be sent into whatever work the Spirit might will. Into the work in which he was sent the power of the Spirit came upon him and he received this very gift of an evangelist which he had coveted. (d.) Acts i. 5, 8. The Baptism of the Holy Spirit always imparts power for service, the services 109to which God calls us. In a certain city was an uneducated boy who was led to Christ. In his very lowly occupation he began witnessing for Jesus. He went on from step to step in Christ's work. My attention was called to him by a gentleman who was interested in him, and who said he would like to have me meet him. The gentleman brought him to Chicago, and I invited him one night to speak in one of our tents. It was in an exceedingly hard neighborhood. Into the same tent an organized mob once came to break up the meeting. It was a difficult audience to hold. The young man began in what appeared to me to be a very commonplace way, and I was afraid I had made a mistake in asking him to speak, but I prayed and watched the audience. There was nothing remarkable in his address as he went on—excepting the bad grammar. But I noticed that all the people were listening. They continued to listen to the end. When I asked if there was any one who wished to accept Christ, people rose in different parts of the tent to signify that they did. Thinking it all over, I told the facts to a man who had known the speaker before. "It is just so wherever he goes" was the reply. What was the explanation? 110This uneducated boy had received the Baptism of the Holy Ghost and had received power. One night at the close of an address on the Baptism of the Holy Spirit, a minister came to me on the platform and said: "I need this power, won't you pray for me?" "Let us kneel right down here now," I replied, and we did. A few weeks after I met a gentleman who had been standing by. "Do you remember," he said "the minister with whom you prayed at New Britain. He went back to his church; his church is packed Sunday evenings, a large part of the audience are young men and he is having conversions right along." He had received the Baptism of the Holy Spirit and "power." (e.) Acts iv. 29–31. The Baptism of the Holy Spirit always imparts boldness in testimony and service. Peter is a notable example of this. Contrast Peter in Acts iv. 8–12 with Peter in Mark xiv. 66–72. Perhaps some one who reads this book has a great desire to speak to others and win them to Christ, but an insuperable timidity stands in the way. If you will only get the Baptism of the Holy Spirit, all that will be overcome.

We are now in a position to define the baptism of the Holy Spirit. The Baptism of the Holy Spirit, is the Spirit of God falling upon 111the believer, taking possession of his faculties, imparting to him gifts not naturally his own, but which qualify him for the service to which God has called him.

2. The necessity of the baptism of the Holy Spirit as a preparation for Christian work.

(1.) In Luke xxiv. 49. Jesus bade the apostles to tarry in Jerusalem until they were "endued with power from on high." These men had been appointed to be witnesses of the life, death and resurrection of Christ. (Luke xxiv. 45–48. Acts; i. 22; x. 39–41.) They had received what would seem to be a splendid and sufficient training for this work. For more than three years they had been to school to the best of teachers, Jesus Himself. They had been eye witnesses of his miracles, death, burial, resurrection and ascension. But there was still one thing needed. And this need was of such vital importance that Jesus would not permit them to enter upon their appointed work until that need had been met. That need was the Baptism of the Holy Spirit. If the apostles with their unparalleled fitting for service, were not permitted to enter that service until all their other training had been supplemented by the Baptism of the Holy Spirit, 112what daring presumption it is for any of us with our inferior training to dare to do it. But this is not all, even Jesus Himself did not enter upon his ministry until specially anointed with the Holy Spirit and with power. (Acts x. 38, comp. Luke iii. 22 and iv. 1, 14). This baptism is an absolutely essential preparation for Christian work. It is either ignorance of the plain requirements of God's word or the most daring presumption on our part when we try to do work for Christ until we know we have been Baptized with the Holy Spirit.

(2.) It is the privilege of every believer to be baptized with the Holy Spirit. This appears from Acts ii. 39, R. V. "To you is the promise and to your children and to all that are afar off, even as many as the Lord our God shall call unto him." The context, the use of the word "promise" in this and the preceding chapter (ch. i. 4; ii. 16, 33.) and the use of the expression "gift of the Holy Spirit" throughout the book, all prove conclusively that "the promise" of this verse means the promise of the Baptism of the Holy Spirit; and the verse tells us that this promise is for all in all ages of the church's history whom God shall call unto him, i. e. for every believer. If we have not this baptism it is our own fault. 113It is for us and we are responsible before God for all the work we might have done, and all the souls we might have won if we were so baptized, and we are guilty to the extent that the work is not done and the souls not won.

3. How can we obtain the Baptism of the Holy Spirit?

We now come to the practical question: how can we obtain this Baptism of the Holy Spirit which is such an absolute necessity in our work for Christ? Fortunately the answer to this question is very plainly stated in the Bible.

(1) "Repent ye and be baptized every one of you in the name of Jesus Christ unto the remission of your sins; and ye shall receive the gift of the Holy Spirit" (Acts ii. 38 R. V.) The first step toward obtaining this Baptism is repentance. Repentance means "a change of mind," a change of mind about sin, about God, and in this case especially (as the context shows) a change of mind about Christ. A real change of mind such as leads to action—to our turning away from all sin, our turning to God, our turning away from rejecting Jesus Christ to accepting Him. The second step is the confession of our renunciation of sin and acceptance of Jesus Christ in God's appointed way 114by baptism in the name of Jesus Christ. The Baptism with the Holy Spirit in at least one instance (Acts x. 44–48) preceded the baptism with water but this was manifestly an exceptional case and God says "repent ye and be baptized every one of you in the

name of Jesus Christ unto the remission of your sins; and ye shall receive the gift of the Holy Spirit," (Acts ii. 38, R. V.)

(2) "The Holy Spirit whom God hath given to them that obey him." (Acts v. 32). The condition of the gift of the Holy Ghost here stated is that we "obey Him." Obedience means more than the mere performance of some of the things that God bids us do. It means the entire surrender of our wills, ourselves and all we have, to Him. It means that we come to Him and say from the heart, "here I am, I am thine, thou hast bought me with a price, I acknowledge thine ownership. Take me, do with me what thou wilt, send me where thou wilt, use me as Thou wilt." This entire yielding of ourselves to God is the condition of our receiving the Baptism of the Holy Spirit, and it is at this point that many fail of this blessing. At the close of a convention a gentleman hurried to the platform and said there was a lady in great distress who wished to speak 115with me. It was an hour before I could get to her, but I found her still in great mental suffering in the intensity of her desire for the Baptism of the Holy Spirit. Others had talked to her but it had seemed to do no good. I sat down behind her and said, "Is your will wholly surrendered?" She did not know. "You wish to be a Christian worker do you not?" "Yes." "Are you willing to go back to Baltimore and be a servant girl if it is God's will?" "No!" "You will never receive this blessing until your own will is wholly laid down." "I can't lay it down." "Would you like to have God lay it down for you?" "Yes." "Well, let us ask Him to do it." We did, he heard the prayer, the will was laid down, the Baptism of the Holy Spirit was received and she went from the church rejoicing.

Obedience means also the doing in all matters great and small, the will of God as revealed in His Word or by His Spirit. Any refusal to do what God bids us do, any conscious doing of what he bids us not do, even in very little matters, is sufficient to shut us out of this blessing. If there is anything no matter how little, that comes up before us to trouble us as we pray over this matter, we should set it right with God at once. Mr. 116Finney tells of one who, in great agony prayed for days for the Baptism of the Holy Spirit but received no answer. At last as she was praying one night she put her hand to her head and took off some little adornment that always came up before her when she prayed and cast it from her. Immediately she received the long desired blessing. It seemed a very little thing but it was a matter of controversy with God and hindered the blessing.

(3.) "How much more shall your Heavenly Father give the Holy Spirit to them that ask Him." (Luke xi. 13.)

(a.) There must be definite prayer for this Baptism. It is often said that the Holy Spirit is already here and that every believer has the Spirit and so we ought not to pray for the Holy Spirit. This argument overlooks the distinction between having the Holy Spirit and having this specific operation of the Holy Spirit. (see 1. 2.) It also contradicts the plain teaching of God's word that He gives "the Holy Spirit to them that ask Him." It is furthermore shown to be fallacious by the fact that the Baptism of the Holy Spirit in the book of Acts was constantly given in connection with and in answer to prayer. (Acts i. 14; ii. 1–4; iv. 31; viii. 15,17.)

(b.) Prayer implies desire. There is no 117real prayer for the Baptism of the Spirit unless there is a deep desire for it. As long as a man thinks he can get along somehow without this blessing, he is not likely to get it; but when a man reaches the place where he feels he must have this no matter what it costs, he is far on the way toward receiving it. Many a minister of the gospel and other worker has been brought to a place where he has felt he could not go on with his ministry without this gift and then the gift has soon followed and the character of his work has been entirely transformed.

(c.) The prayer to be effectual must be in faith (Mark xi. 24). James says in regard to the prayer for wisdom, "Let him ask in faith, nothing wavering. For he that wavereth is like a wave of sea driven with the wind and tossed. For let not that man think that he shall receive anything of the Lord." (Jas. i. 6, 7.) The same principle, of course, holds in regard to the prayer for the Holy Spirit. It is at this very point that many miss the blessing. How to approach God in faith is clearly taught by 1 Jno. v. 14, 15. "This is the confidence that we have in Him, that, if we ask anything according to his will He heareth us, and if we know that he hear us whatsoever 118we ask, we know that we have the petitions that we desired of him." When we ask Him for the Baptism of the Holy Spirit we know that we have asked something according to His will for it is definitely promised in His word. Therefore we know that "He heareth us; and if we know that He hear us we know that we have the petition" which we have asked of him. As soon then as I am sure I have met the conditions stated above of the gift of the Holy Spirit, and asked it of God I have a right to count this blessing mine—the prayer is heard and I have the petition I asked of him—and get up and enter into my work assured that in my work will be seen the Spirit's power. "But," some one will say, "shall we expect no manifestations?" Yes, but where? In service. When I know on the authority of God's word that my prayer is heard, I have the right to enter upon any service to which He calls me and confidently expect the manifestation of the Spirit's power in that service. It is a mistake to wait or look for, as so many do, the manifestation in electric shocks or peculiar emotional experiences. They may and often do accompany the Baptism of the Holy Spirit. But the Bible clearly teaches us (i Cor. xii. 4–11) that the place to 119look for manifestations, is in service and the most important, reliable and scriptural manifestations are found in our work. "Must we not wait," it may be asked, "until we know that we have received the baptism of the Holy Spirit?" Most assuredly, but how are we to know? The same way in which we know we are saved, by the testimony of God's word. When I know I have met the conditions and have asked this gift which is "according to his will" I know by God's word

(1 Jno. v. 14, 15.) that my prayer is heard, and that I have the petition I desired of him. I have a right to arise with no other evidence than the all–sufficient evidence of God's word, and enter into the service to which God calls me. "Did not the early disciples wait ten days?" it may again be asked. Yes, and the reason why is clearly given in Acts ii. 1.—"When the day of Pentecost was fully come." In the O. T. types the day of Pentecost had been appointed as the day in God's economy for the first giving of the Holy Spirit and the offering of the first–fruits (the church) and so the Holy Spirit could not be given until that day. (Lev. xxiii. 9–17.) But after the Spirit was once given we find no protracted period of waiting on the part of those who sought this blessing. (Acts 120iv. 31; viii. 15, 17; ix. 17, 20; xix. 6.) Men are obliged to wait to–day, but it is only because they have not met the conditions, or do not believe and claim the blessing simply on the Word of God. The moment we meet the conditions and claim the blessing it is ours. (Mark xi. 24 R.V.) Any child of God may lay down this book, meet the conditions, ask the blessing, claim it and have it. In a Students' Summer School at Lake Geneva after a talk by F. B. Meyer on the Baptism of the Holy Spirit, a student remained to talk with me. He said he had heard of this before and had been seeking it for months but could not get it. I found his will was not surrendered, but that was soon settled. Then I said, "Let us kneel down and ask God for the Baptism of the Holy Spirit." He did so. Was that petition "according to his will?" I asked. "Yes." "Was the prayer heard?" After some hesitation, "It must have been." "Have you what you asked of Him?" "I don't feel it." I read 1 Jno. v. 15 from the Bible that lay open before us: "If we know that he hears us, whatsoever we ask, we know that we have the petition we desired of him." "Was the prayer heard?" "Yes." "Have you what you asked?" "I must have; for God says so." We arose and 121soon separated. Going back to the school in a few days I met the young man again. His face was now all aglow and he knew he had received what at first he took upon the bare word of God.

4. The Repetition of the Baptism of the Holy Spirit.

One thing more needs to be said before we leave this subject. The Baptism of the Holy Spirit is an experience that needs frequent repeating. This appears from a comparison of Acts ii. 4—where Peter with others was filled with the Holy Spirit—with Acts iv. 8.—where Peter was filled again,—and with Acts iv. 31 where Peter with others was filled yet again. A new filling is needed and should be sought for each new emergency of Christian service. There are many who once knew experimentally what the Baptism of the Holy Spirit meant who are trying to work to–day in the power of that old experience and are working without God. They need and must have a new Baptism before God can use them.

www.ingramcontent.com/pod-product-compliance
Lightning Source LLC
Chambersburg PA
CBHW071817190726
48292CB00008B/2870

* 9 7 8 1 9 5 1 4 9 7 1 5 6 *